18—

S0-BTR-010

ArtScroll Series®

Rabbi Nosson Scherman / Rabbi Meir Zlotowitz
General Editors

MAKING
little
THINGS
COUNT

Published by

Mesorah Publications, ltd

& BIG THINGS BETTER

AVI SHULMAN

FIRST EDITION
First Impression ... April 2001

Published and Distributed by
MESORAH PUBLICATIONS, LTD.
4401 Second Avenue / Brooklyn, N.Y 11232

Distributed in Europe by
LEHMANNS
Unit E, Viking Industrial Park
Rolling Mill Road
Jarrow, Tyne & Wear, NE32 3DP
England

Distributed in Australia and New Zealand by
GOLDS WORLD OF JUDAICA
3-13 William Street
Balaclava, Melbourne 3183
Victoria Australia

Distributed in Israel by
SIFRIATI / A. GITLER
6 Hayarkon Street
Bnei Brak 51127

Distributed in South Africa by
KOLLEL BOOKSHOP
Shop 8A Norwood Hypermarket
Norwood 2196, Johannesburg, South Africa

ARTSCROLL SERIES®
MAKING LITTLE THINGS COUNT & BIG THINGS BETTER
© *Copyright 2001, by* MESORAH PUBLICATIONS, Ltd.
4401 Second Avenue / Brooklyn, N.Y. 11232 / (718) 921-9000 / www.artscroll.com

---

ALL RIGHTS RESERVED
The text, prefatory and associated textual contents and introductions
— including the typographic layout, cover artwork and ornamental graphics —
have been designed, edited and revised as to content, form and style.

No part of this book may be reproduced
IN ANY FORM, PHOTOCOPYING, OR COMPUTER RETRIEVAL SYSTEMS
— even for personal use without written permission from
the copyright holder, Mesorah Publications Ltd.
except by a reviewer who wishes to quote brief passages
in connection with a review written for inclusion in magazines or newspapers.

THE RIGHTS OF THE COPYRIGHT HOLDER WILL BE STRICTLY ENFORCED.

ISBN:
1-57819-491-1 (hard cover)
1-57819-492-X (paperback)

Typography by CompuScribe at ArtScroll Studios, Ltd.
Printed in the United States of America by Noble Book Press Corp.
Bound by Sefercraft, Quality Bookbinders, Ltd., Brooklyn N.Y. 11232

This book is dedicated to the loving
memory of
Rabbi Dov Greenbaum זצ״ל

who was dean of the Yeshiva of Spring Valley for
three decades until his *petirah* on Tishah B'Av תשמ״ב.
During these years Rabbi Greenbaum spearheaded the
phenomenal growth of the Monsey community into becoming a unique Torah community.

What was apparent was the fact that the Rabbi was
my good friend, neighbor, employee, principal to my
children, and shul benchmate. What was not as readily apparent was that he was also my teacher, mentor,
and a major inspiration.

His education philosophy which was the legacy of his
sainted father-in-law Rabbi Shraga Feivel Mendlowitz
זצ״ל created the flagship yeshivah which became the
model for *chinuch*.

An appreciation of Rabbi Greenbaum appears in
the last section of this book.

TORAH UMESORAH
תורה ומסורה

The National Society for
Hebrew Day Schools

COMMITTING GENERATIONS TO TORAH

Rosh Chodesh Iyar, 5761

The publication of a new book by Reb Avi Shulman is indeed an occasion for celebration in the world of Torah Chinuch.

So many people have told me that Reb Avi's lectures and writings have literally changed their lives. Torah Chinuch is all about changing lives.

Reb Avi's Torah wisdom and his ability to express and convey his profound thoughts directly to the hearts and minds of his audience is truly extraordinary.

We look forward to many years of his wisdom, his teaching, and his enormous contribution to Torah Chinuch.

Sincerely,

Rabbi Joshua Fishman
Executive Vice President

160 BROADWAY, 4th Fl.

NEW YORK, NY 10038

TEL: (212) 227-1000

FAX: (212) 406-6934

E-mail: umesorah @ aol.com

TABLE OF CONTENTS

	Introduction	11
	Thank You	17
1.	The Mountain	19
2.	A Clean Slate — Part One	23
3.	A Clean Slate — Part Two	27
4.	Everything counts	31
5.	Write a Book	35
6.	A Family Reunion	39
7.	A Note to the Rebbe	43
8.	A Radio Tower	47
9.	Give Me More, More & More	51
10.	Let Her Stew for a Few Days	55
11.	The Time Box — Part One	59
12.	The Time Box — Part Two	63
13.	Are You Listening?	67
14.	Erev Shabbos Delight	71
15.	How to Read a Book	75
16.	If It Ain't Broke	79
17.	What Is Your Paradigm?	83
18.	The Walk Home	87
19.	Flying Geese	91
20.	Kinder Words	95

21.	Vidalia Onions	99
22.	Supper Time	103
23.	Guilt	107
24.	The Telephone — Part One	111
25.	The Telephone — Part Two	115
26.	Emergancies	120
27.	Coping — Part One	126
28.	Coping — Part Two	130
29.	Homework — Part One	134
30.	Homework — Part Two	138
31.	Grandparents	142
32.	Retired	146
33.	A New Phenomenon	150
34.	Creativity — Part One	155
35.	Creativity — Part Two	159
36.	Driving — Part One	164
37.	Driving — Part Two	169
38.	Driving — Part Three	174
39.	Driving — Part Four	178
40.	Driving — Part Five	182
41.	A good Fight	187
42.	Whisper Power	191
	In Appreciation	195

MAKING LITTLE THINGS COUNT & BIG THINGS BETTER

This is a unique book ... 42 diverse and pertinent chapters ... each providing about ten minutes of stimulating and rewarding reading .... each inspiring your own thought, setting you on a positive course of immediately useful ideas .... so that you may build the productive, fulfilling life you want.

The purpose of this book is to stimulate constructive thoughts, to give you thoughts, improved direction, and greater substance, and to provide the kind of motivational thinking which will enable you to deal successfully with yourself, with others, and with any difficulties which arise.

INTRODUCTION

Thoughts are where it is at.

Why?

Because our thoughts determine what we think of ourselves, how we perceive our abilities, how we react to what happens to us, and what we hope to accomplish in life.

To a thinking person ...

... speech begins with thoughts;

... action begins with thoughts;

... religious adherence depends on thoughts;

... change is prefaced by thoughts;

... we learn from our mistakes by thoughts;

... relationship with others depends on thoughts;

... happiness depends on thoughts.

Thoughts are the buildings blocks of our lives because how a man behaves outwardly is but the expression of his inner thoughts.

There is no profound or deep philosophy in this book; rather it is replete with easy to understand thoughts that all enjoy the common denominator of being Thoughts to Build On.

Each brief chapter can be read in just a few minutes and hopefully will give you a different, stimulating thought to mull over in your mind, and to discuss with your family to enhance your enjoyment of this book, I suggest you use it as a springboard for conversation with your family. Open to almost any chapter and ask, "What would you say about this topic," or "How would you solve this problem?" This should lead to an exciting discussion. You may agree or disagree with a specific approach or suggestion; that really is not important. What is important is that you do independent thinking on the topic at hand and discuss it.

We have chosen three general topics for this book: Parenting, Teaching, and Personal Growth.

Parenting for many, especially for those with large families, is a subject that occupies a disproportionate amount of time, energy, and worry. Until recently, parenting skills were thought to arrive automatically along with the firstborn child's birth certificate. We were supposed to do "what came naturally," which probably meant we were to do what our parents did; and if we had a problem on occasion, a quick question to Grandmother would provide all the direction needed.

In the last few decades we have been coming to grips with the reality that although our own parenting instincts are adequate most of the time, there are enough times when we need guidance from others. Whether it is because of changing times, the family size, the working mother, the influence of the media, or any or all of the above, the bottom line is that parenting has become a subject to which all of us should pay full attention. I hope that I have presented some positive and useful ideas — mostly borrowed — for your consideration.

As is well known, the most effective way to teach is by example. People learn more from what you do than from what you say. Therefore, teaching is not limited to the *rebbi*, the *morah*, or the teacher standing in front of the classroom; rather I have included ideas and suggestions for all of us. In truth, all of us in one way or another are teachers. The *rebbi* teaches formally in the classroom, the rabbi teaches in his sermons and in adult classes, and the parent teaches in casual discussions — but all of us teach. So the ideas and suggestions offered here will hopefully be of interest to everyone.

Personal growth is a "catchall" phrase that is meant to include almost anything that will make us better, that will stimulate growth, that will bring us closer to achieving our many objectives.

In our yeshivah days we would hear the phrase "*shteigen in lernin* or *shteigen in middos*" which, loosely translated, means "to grow, to improve in learning or *middos*." We can recall our *Rosh Hayeshivah, Rebbi,* and *Mashgiach* imploring, urging, or challenging — and on occasion demanding of us — to improve! Their message was: "Strive to make this week more productive than last week; strive to make your ethical behavior more refined than last month; strive to make your *davening* this quarter more meaningful than last quarter."

Those of us who leave the walls of the yeshivah can wait in vain for years for someone to challenge us to *shteig.* The honest truth is that most of us have to challenge ourselves if we want to achieve.

Just as the entry-level office worker is initially accountable to a boss and, as he goes up the corporate ladder, increasingly accountable to himself, so each of us should become increasingly more self-accountable as we mature.

These articles are the result of prodding by Rabbi Joshua Fishman, Executive Vice President of Torah Umesorah. He recognized the need for parents and teachers to discuss relevant topics, and during the years that I was a Torah Umesorah staff member he continually urged me to write.

Rabbi Yaakov Rajchenbach in his first year as president of Torah Umesorah suggested that these articles be published in a weekly column in the Yated Ne'eman.

I am grateful to Rabbi Fishman, Rabbi Rajchenbach, and Rabbi Pinchos Lipschutz, publisher of Yated Ne'eman, for their encouragement and support.

I would like to thank Rabbis Meir Zlotowitz and Nosson Scherman, both lifelong friends, Reb Sheah Brander, and all the ArtScroll-Mesorah organization. All of us owe them an enormous debt of gratitude, because they have provided us with insights into *tefillah*, *Tanach*, Talmud, and Jewish history and thought, that have immeasurably enhanced everyone's learning opportunities.

I would also like to thank Rabbi and Mrs. Yisroel Flam, and my wife Erica for their help.

THANK YOU

First, I wish to express profound gratitude to Hashem for having given me so much: life, health, talents, opportunities, a very special family, friends, and community. I am especially blessed to have always been associated with *Roshei HaYeshivos, Rabbanim, Bnei Torah,* and Torah personalities.

My father's *zt"l yiras shamayim,* integrity, and dedication to Torah is a constant inspiration to me. No doubt, the benevolence Hashem grants me is due to *zechus avos,* my parents' merits.

I want to express appreciation to the very special people who over the last years have embraced me with concern, support, and true friendship. Each in his or her own way, in the right time, has helped and inspired me. In many ways, this book is the product of what I have learned from them.

My family: my wife Erica, our children, and their extended families.

My Torah Umesorah family: with special appreciation to Rabbi Joshua Fishman.

My Mercaz family: with special appreciation to Rabbis Wein and Joel Kramer.

My Aish Dos family: with special appreciation to Rabbi Dovid Bernstein.

My ArtScroll family, my Bais Shraga family, my Yeshiva of Spring Valley family, My Daf Yomi family, my *Rebbis* and *chavrusos,* all my good friends, my "boys club." A special appreciation to Michael Rothschild: a tremendous thank-you.

1

THE MOUNTAIN

I was invited to spend a Shabbos as the guest of the Seattle *kollel,* a *kollel* which was the fruit of four Torah Umesorah S.E.E.D. programs.

There is much to be said and written about the unique Seattle Jewish community in general, and the accomplishments of the *kollel* in particular. There are lessons of life-long friendship, organizational *shalom bayis,* and dedicated people. I want to share a lesson I learned from *The Mountain.*

Seventy miles to the south of Seattle lies Mt. Rainier, one of the tallest mountains in North America. It stands 14,410-feet high, and its year–round snowcapped peaks can be clearly seen for miles around. Mt. Rainier is a dominant force in the state of Washington; in fact, its picture is featured on the license plates. When a house is built on a hill in Seattle, the architect tries to position the major living areas to face south, and will often include floor–to–ceiling glass walls to view The Mountain.

We drove to Mt. Rainier and were overwhelmed by the beauty the Almighty vested in the Northwest. All around the base of the mountain, for a fifty-mile radius, there are tall evergreen trees that flourish in the mild climate and snow–fed streams. Magnificent lakes, rivers, and miles of trails make this area one of the most desirable in the country for camping and hiking.

After an exciting day at The Mountain, we came back to the city and I went to *Minchah.* After *davening* I was sharing my excitement with a group of local residents and another guest also from back east. After briefly listening to my description, the guest said, "I wonder if I could get a Coca-Cola sign on top of The

Mountain. That would be a great advertisement!"

Suddenly the group, which had been talkative and congenial, became quiet and cold. The out-of-towner immediately realized he had said something inappropriate and apologized by saying, "I was only kidding about the sign. It was just a joke."

One of the locals looked at him, and, after what seemed like a very long time, quietly said, "Sir, we don't joke about *The Mountain!*"

That caught my attention. It meant that because we recognize the unique beauty of this gift, because we appreciate the quality of life we enjoy because of the income from the lumber and tourist industries, The Mountain is *too special to joke about!*

It set me thinking about the phrase, "It's just a joke." We all enjoy an appropriate joke, and a good *kibbitz* has become a matter of routine. These oil the wheels of social interaction and inject a light touch to otherwise weighty conversation.

There was a time when certain people were considered too prominent, and certain subjects too sacred for jest. Over the past fifty years, the media has eroded respect for anyone or anything to the point where, in

Western culture today, there is nothing about which we cannot joke.

Yet we, as Torah–observant Jews, have to realize that our values are different. There truly are people and subjects about which *any joke is inappropriate*. Our parents; Torah, its teachers, students, and *yeshivos; mitzvos* and those who observe them — all are unique gifts from the Almighty. They enrich our quality of life, give meaning, purpose, and eternity to our actions, and afford us the opportunity to live a fulfilled life . . . all too special to joke about!

"We don't joke about *The Mountain*" is a good reminder that even jest has its limitations.

2

A CLEAN SLATE

Part One

The beginning of anything new is usually accompanied by a refreshing burst of enthusiasm, an excitement that holds out a promise that this project will be different and better than anything before.

The beginning of a new school year should hold out the exact same promise. This year the student will try harder, will do better in every subject. A new teacher, a new classroom, different textbooks, and new clothing all say

to the student, "This year can be more productive than last year."

Here are several suggestions that may help
reinforce this wonderful enthusiasm and keep
it going.

1. SET POSITIVE BUT REALISTIC EXPECTATIONS.

For the student who has educational,
behavioral, or social difficulties in school, it is
especially important to approach the new
school term expecting to work toward over-
coming last year's problem. This does not
mean that the student who was deficient in
math should expect to become a top math
student (although, surprisingly, that can
happen too) ; the student should say to himself, "I can do better. This new school term I
will listen more actively in class, do my
homework with greater concentration,
behave with more maturity, and pursue my
relationships with greater sensitivity." The
goal is not for the child to become the perfect
student in one quantum leap, but rather to
make significant strides in the right direction.

An open, nonconfrontational discussion to
lay out the opportunities of the new school

year and your realistic expectations will do much for your child.

2. NURTURE GROWTH EVEN WHEN YOU DO NOT SEE IT.

The growth of a child presents two problems for parents.

The first is that growth is often imperceptible. A slight increase in attentiveness may not be noticed by a teacher, and it may take months (or years) until it is reflected in a measurable grade. The child's becoming "somewhat more serious" is a small nuance that can easily be lost in the tumult of everything else going on in his day; but these incremental gains represent growth. Just as a small plant needs to be nurtured whether or not we can see it growing, the student needs positive nurturing even when we do not see him grow!

The teacher or parent who expects growth to occur in spurts or giant steps will be disappointed. No doubt, when improvement is slow and small, the child is also frustrated, and at this time he needs the nurturing even more.

The second problem is that we tend to continue to see the child the way he always was. Parents often fail to acknowledge the growth that has taken place and still view the child as the youngster he or she was last year.

3. SHOW THE CHILD THAT NONSCHOLASTIC GROWTH CAN HELP HIM IN SCHOOLWORK.

While we think of school as the major educational influence on our child, there are many nonschool activities that help him grow.

For example, when a 12 year-old goes to sleep-away camp for the first time and does very well, it is the result of many newly acquired skills, all having personal growth as a common denominator.

We can go one step further by getting the following message across: "Just as you have learned new skills this summer, you can learn new skills in school."

I have a friend who told me that a three-day mountain-climbing expedition when he was sixteen years old was the turning point in his classroom learning because the leader of the group kept saying over and over again, "If you can learn to climb this next ridge, you can learn anything!" Pride in accomplishing a new skill acted as a reinforcement for other efforts in the boy's life.

3

A CLEAN SLATE

Part Two

*I*n the last chapter we discussed the opportunity afforded by a clean slate at the beginning of the year, and three tools for helping the student start the new school term more efficiently. We continue our discussion.

4. SET HOME-STUDY GUIDELINES.

The beginning of a new year is a wonderful time to set guidelines for homework. You and your child may benefit greatly from a discussion (where both participants listen, in addition to expressing their point of view) about when homework should be done, the time allotted to it, and how it will be supervised. Ask the child what he/she would consider fair and then determine whether the two of you can reach some agreement. How about from 8 to 9 o'clock every night? What about telephone calls? What about friends coming over?

At this point you and your child are non-confrontational, both of you are on the same side, and the subject may be easier to discuss.

5. SET REVIEW DATES.

Consult a calendar now and write down, while you are still enthusiastic about doing a great job, specific dates when both parents will review progress with each child.

For example, four weeks after the holidays might be the first time to review all the subjects, Hebrew and secular, teacher sheets, tests, and workbooks.

In one hour, parents who give a child full attention will not only get a very good idea of how well the child is doing in each subject, but will also teach the child a more important lesson: that they are intensely interested in his work.

This method is so much better than relying on the parent-teacher meeting alone, because your own meeting with your child is private and personal, and demonstrates real concern. You may discover a problem that can easily be corrected at the beginning of the school year.

It is also important to develop an open line of communication with the teacher.

6. BRICK BY BRICK, DAY BY DAY

In our fast-moving world, where news is instantaneous, letters are faxed, and travel is at jet speed, we become impatient with anything slow — even growth.

Compare the educational process to the building of a house. A bricklayer positions one brick at a time in building a house, and the student learns one fact, acquires one skill or perfects one personality trait in his development.

The work the student does today may seem inconsequential. Does the bricklayer reason that since he is laying only a few bricks today, he can place them carelessly? Obviously not. He knows that the work is cumulative. He knows that the totality of the job will depend on how well each row of bricks is placed. So too, we must try to do today's work as best we can.

This week's personal improvement may seem imperceptible, but just as bricks which are meticulously laid daily soon become a strong wall, then a beautiful building, a lesson learned today, a good deed done, and a temptation over-come soon build an individual of knowledge and character.

The opening of school coincides with the month of Elul – traditionally dedicated to introspection and self-improvement. This is a wonderful time to evaluate the beginning of our New Year. It can also enable us to serve as instructional role models for our children to teach them how to prepare for their new school year.

4

EVERYTHING COUNTS

*M*en do not stumble over mountains; they stumble over molehills. When we come to major crossroads in our lives, the direction we choose can set the course for years to come. Selecting a spouse, a career, an education, or even the neighborhood we live in is so important that we are usually careful to get adequate guidance and scrupulously pursue our options before arriving at a decision.

Surprisingly, however, it is the hundreds of seemingly insignificant choices that we make every day that truly shape our lives.

As an example, whether we eat a healthy breakfast or just a cup of coffee; whether lunch includes fruit or vegetables; and whether we eat too much red meat at supper are not by themselves very momentous choices. Really, how much can one healthy meal add to our general well-being, and how much harm can just one sandwich do? We convince ourselves that the benefit or harm from one meal is really very little . . . and that thought becomes our nemesis.

Since the consequences of a small choice are not readily discernible, we are often fooled into thinking "it doesn't count," but the truth is that it does count, or as a friend of mine often says, "Everything counts."

Here is an interesting way to teach the concept "everything counts" to a young person. Hand him a sheet of 8½ x 11 paper and ask, "Does this sheet of paper weigh anything?" The answer obviously is, "No, it doesn't weigh anything." If you have a kitchen or bathroom scale, you can place a sheet of paper on it, and the scale will not register any change.

But place a ream of 500 sheets of the same paper on the scale, and it weighs four or five pounds. The fact is that each sheet of paper does, of course, weigh something – if not, then 500 times zero would still be zero, not five pounds. It is just that on our scales such a miniscule weight is negigible and does not register.

The major lesson to be learned from this experiment is that whether or not our scales register the weight of one sheet of paper is not the criterion – each piece of paper does weigh something, and it contributes to the total.

Likewise, whether or not our scales, or society's scales, register a single act as detrimental really does not make a difference — because everything counts.

Every day we are faced with hundreds of choices. Do I get up now or later? Will I be pleasant or grouchy? Will I be early or late? Will I daven intently or not? Will I give *tzedakah* graciously or not at all? As I travel to work, will I use my time productively? Will I speak *lashon hara* or not?

On a child's level the choices can include the following: Will I listen to today's lesson? Will I be the best in my class or be a troublemaker? Will I play nicely with my friends?

The list of choices continues as the day proceeds. Decisions about relationships, honest fulfillment of *mitzvos*, and use of time confront us to the very last moment before we fall asleep.

It is these decisions – the small molehills – that often trip us. We are aware of the far-reaching importance of the big decisions, but in the small, seemingly unimportant decisions, we are frequently fooled. Once we are aware that "everything counts" and that the cumulative effect of seemingly insignificant choices can be enormous, we will pay more attention to all our choices.

5

WRITE A BOOK

Years ago I read a letter written by an older man advising his younger reader to "write a book" because, he explained, "a book is really all that we can leave to our future generations."

At that time I thought the advice was ridiculous. Many of us do not have anything important to say, and many of us cannot express our thoughts clearly. Moreover, most of us do not possess the ability to put these thoughts down on paper.

However, over the years, I have developed a new understanding of the subject and would like to share it.

Tatti's Vertlach

Ever since the children could remember, Father – Tatti, as they affectionately called him – always had a few *divrei Torah* or *vertlach* on each *parashah*. In the early years when the children were young, Tatti would deliver these Torah thoughts to a bunch of disinterested children who could not wait to finish the *seudah* and go out to play. As the children grew older, they recognized and remembered each week's *vertlach* and, like meeting a long-lost friend, relished hearing them again.

One by one the children married, and soon it was their young sons and daughters who sat at Zeide and Bubby's Shabbos table, squirming when these same Torah thoughts were discussed.

Notwithstanding the reams of *parashah* sheets the children and grandchildren now bring to the Shabbos table, notwithstanding the scores of *sefarim* that offer us the "best *vertlach*," Tatti's or Zeide's *vertlach* have a special place in the family.

To Tatti or Zeide we give this advice: Write down a few favorite *vertlach* from each *parashah*, have them typed and then photo-copied and assembled into a small booklet. Your children and grandchildren may refer to it each Shabbos and will relish the special memories. These *vertlach* bind you and your family to the *dvar* Torah for posterity.

As an aside, I gave this advice to a friend of mine who became so involved in writing his insights on the *parashah* that he published a formidable *sefer* on *Bereishis* and *Shemos*. We never know where a good idea can take us.

Write your own observations of life

Some of us find it helpful to formulate our thoughts and observations in writing. We can set the paper aside for a time, review, edit, change, and discuss it.

We may want to share events that were meaningful to us with our children and grandchildren and future generations. Looking back on life now, understanding what occurred ten, twenty, or thirty years ago, puts life into perspective. The message here is: Even if we do not understand it all now, we may understand it later. We may want to write about people who inspired us. Many of us have had the good fortune to have a mentor enter our lives just at the time we needed it most. If you had such a friend, it would be appropriate to describe how this person became your mentor and the value of his influence. Another topic is the history of our family. Whatever family history we can remember or trace may be of great interest to someone in the future. Finally, we can write about values that have a special place in our hearts. We can go further and consider a message or mission statement for future generations. What message would you want to share with them?

Contrary to everything you learned in English 101, your book does not have to be a literary masterpiece; it does not require major themes or any other devices used by authors. Your book should reflect you!

6

A FAMILY REUNION

We went to visit friends from out of town and unexpectedly found ourselves in the midst of a full-fledged family reunion.

Six siblings and their respective spouses, all in their late 50's/60's were spending a Shabbos together in the home of one sister, reminiscing and enjoying each other's company.

While each sibling occasionally visited with a brother or sister and they all came together at *simchahs*, it was the fact that they made the opportunity to come together for a Shabbos when there was no *simchah* that made this occasion so special. There was no agenda to follow, no program to keep to, no outsiders to intrude (no children for whom Chaim would have to be Uncle Chaim with the special status the title implied). There was no one to impress, no reason to create a facade. Rather, the Shabbos was totally natural, as if each of them had said, "We are here just to enjoy our own company."

I found it refreshing that the six couples chose to spend Shabbos in the home of a sibling rather than in a hotel. Spending the Shabbos in a sibling's home meant *davening* where their host *davened*, going to *shiurim* with him or her, and in many other ways becoming for those two days part of the host sibling's life-style.

Here are some additional observations:

- All six siblings and their spouses escaped Hitler *Yemach Shemo* by one means or another.

- All six were in the same religious sphere — they were *Shomer Shabbos*, attended *shiurim* and had children who went to yeshivah.

- All were in the same general financial sphere. The husbands and wives were successful in business or their profession.

Although some lived out of town, they came in for this Shabbos, making an obvious statement that this was high on their list of priorities.

We find in *Nach* the expression *zevach mishpachah,* a family festivity. We usually associate that with a Yom Tov or *simchah,* and in our minds we imagine a long table surrounded by children and grandchildren adorned in the finest clothing, eating, singing, saying *divrei Torah* in honor of the Yom Tov. That is surely the meaning of the phrase. However, there are those who say that the dynamics of zevach mashpachah apply even in just a family get-together!

Family life is under attack today as never before in the history of the world. Even in our Torah world, married children move to other communities hundreds or thousands of miles away if an opportunity arises. Yet the family is one of the most powerful forces that keep children loyal to parents' values. A close family is emotionally fulfilling and a safety net in times of crisis.

Family closeness does not just happen. It requires a plan, a dedication, an overriding desire to make it happen. It requires instilling in children the value of family while they are young, creating exciting "family" times, trips, outings, picnics, projects, when "family togetherness" is fostered.

One winter, friends of mine found themselves hosting a *melaveh malkah* every second week. They decided to surprise their family by making a *melaveh malkah* just for their own children, who were their "special guests." The children remember it as a high point decades later.

Often we take the family for granted. Perhaps it would be to our benefit to give consideration as to how to make it special.

7

A NOTE TO THE REBBI

If any reader wants to publish a guaranteed best-seller, all he or she has to do is collect notes that children bring to school to excuse their absence. Publish this collection and you will "have it made."

A note to the *rebbi* (and we use the word *rebbi* to include *moros* and teachers) is one of a limited means of communication between parents and teacher.

In every note sent to the *rebbi* there are

indeed actually several messages being sent:

1. The actual message: "Chaim had fever yesterday and couldn't come to school."
2. It tells what the writer of the note thinks of the *rebbi*.
3. It tells what the children think the parent thinks of the rebbi.

When the *rebbi* is perceived as the person who conveys Torah text, Torah values, and education to the child – and this applies to a rebbe who teaches *Gemara* as well as one who teaches *Aleph-Beis* (and this also pertains to secular teachers) – there is an implied respect which is expressed in many subtle ways.

Writing a note to the *rebbi* may be a seemingly insignificant, routine act. Visualize a mother preparing to send her children out to a school bus or carpool when suddenly little Rochel says, "Oh, I just remembered. I need a note for yesterday . . ." The fact that the harried mother can dismiss this note so easily is the very reason that it offers a great opportunity to teach our important lesson.

The parent who dashes off a thoughtless, perfunctory scribble on a scrap of paper is at best missing the opportunity... or at worst reinforcing the message of casualness, friendly, "take-for-granted" disrespect.

How would you, as a *rebbi,* react to the following note explaining a child's absence?

Cute, funny... perhaps. Respectful... hardly.

How would you, as a *rebbi* react to a note on a piece of paper that is literally 1x2 inches?

How would you, as a *rebbi,* respond to a note that says, "Please excuse my son for not being in school yesterday"?

I remember when I was a *rebbi* receiving a carefully handwritten letter on a sheet of expensive personal stationery. The letter, whose tone was friendly yet respectful, addressed me in full title and came in a sealed envelope on which was written a full address.

It may have taken the father a few minutes

to write the letter, but the message to both the student and myself lasted decades!

The unwritten message that I read was: You, *Rebbi*, are very important to my son, to me, to us. The absence was unavoidable, but it was nevertheless a real loss for which I am sorry. Thank you, *Rebbi*, for teaching my son."

Imagine little Chaim saying, " Tatti, I need a note." The father finds an appropriate piece of stationery, spends some time considering how to address the *rebbi*, carefully begins to write. Chaim is impatiently watching every move. "Come on, Tatti, "m in a hurry! Please just say I was sick!"

The father laboriously writes the letter, addresses the envelope, and seals it. Chaim's father does not have to make a speech about the importance of a *rebbi*. The note says it all.

8

A RADIO TOWER

*N*ear the Detroit *kollel* there is a 650-foot-high radio tower that dominates an entire square block. To support and stabilize the tower, at every hundred feet on the tower there are three guy wires stretching down to large anchors cemented into the ground. Each of the eighteen guy wires is one inch thick and is comprised of dozens of strands of tightly coiled wires. It is an engineering feat, and truly an impressive sight.

I was walking near the tower one day when an interesting thought occurred to me. What would happen if someone cut each of the guy wires, yet the tower still remained standing? A few hours later, a large truck might rumble by the nearby highway, and the tower would come crashing down.

What caused the tower to fall?

The casual observer would immediately say, "I saw the truck rumble by and cause the tower to fall. I saw it happen with my own eyes. Cause and effect."

The more astute person, and surely anyone trained as an engineer, architect, or scientist, would say, "The truck was merely incidental. The person who cut the supporting wires so weakened the tower that it actually crashed when the wires were cut. The truck merely knocked over an 'empty shell.'"

Reb Chaim Volozhin states in *Nefesh HaChaim* that we are mistaken if we think that Nevuchadnetzar and Titus caused any (actual) spiritual damage when they destroyed the *Beis HaMikdash*. These wicked men have no portion in the world above, and their activities do not reach there at all. It was the sins of *Klal Yisrael* that weakened their spirituality to the point where Nevuchadnetzar and Titus were able to destroy the "wood and stones" of the *Beis HaMikdash*.

The computer acronym "wysiwyg" (what you see is what you get) can easily lead us to believe as well that what we see is really what happened. Sometimes. But other times what we see is only one side of the story, and we need the expertise of *Chazal* to explain to us what really happened.

There are scores of such stories and situations. *Mechiras Yosef* — the brothers selling Yosef — and the story of Purim are two that immediately come to mind, where an understanding of what really happened is vastly different from what the casual reader may believe. If we do not develop understanding but merely rely on the superficial facts, we are doomed to misunderstanding and grave error.

As parents and teachers it behooves us to use every opportunity to teach our children not to immediately accept the apparent, surface reason for an incident or phenomenon. Too often what we see at first glance is artificial and illusory. We should use the Almighty's gift to us – our ability to think, question, and probe, to ask knowledgeable people until we uncover the genuine and authentic reasons. This lesson can help our children avoid much disillusionment and heartbreak.

This is a heavy subject and deserves more discussion. However, without trivializing it, I want to share a cute story. I shared a ride with a family, and as we drove out of the city we noticed two men nonchalantly walking along the road. The young son of my friend asked, "Why are these men just walking? Why aren't they working?" As a response, the father challenged the family to think of different ways that these men could actually be doing their work as they walked. I was amazed at some of the creative answers and it taught me you can use almost any situation to look beyond the obvious.

9

GIVE ME MORE, MORE AND MORE

A tired, but very happy grandmother finally arrives at the home of her son, daughter-in-law and grandchildren and is greeted by an anxious and excited family. "Bubby, what did you bring us?" The chorus of voices ring out!

"What did you bring us?"

We are not describing a family of poor, impoverished, undernourished children. On the contrary, each child is well fed, nicely clothed, and supplied with a closet full of toys – board games, electronic games, and sports equipment that would gladden the heart of any toy-store owner.

Yet the cry is for more.

We know very well that the latest toy will only hold their attention for a few moments, but anyway, "We want more."

We adults know that there is really no need for another toy or game, yet we allow ourselves to fall into the trap. Why?

First, coming to a house with a loaded bag of toys insures us instant approval and love. "Wow, look at what Bubby brought" is equated with "They love me."

We all know that gifts do not buy love, but it feels so good to fool ourselves. "See how happy the children are. They really love me."

Second, the children expect it, and we do not want to disappoint them.

Third, how can a guest not bring something?

Before we discuss the questions at hand, allow me to share a story.

A friend of mine tells his children when he comes home from a business trip, "I brought you some interesting stories about the places I visited." At supper he takes out picture postcards, newspapers, pictures, and inexpensive memorabilia, and tells them about his experiences in the city or country he visited. His stories make the experience so real that years later when a child visited the city his father had described, he had a feeling of déjà vu.

What gift did the father bring his children from each trip? The gift of time, the gift of concern, the gift of the message: "I'm interested in you. I was thinking of you while I was away." Of course children need gifts and toys; we will try to address this issue in a future article. The purpose of this discussion is to question the wisdom or folly of training children to expect a gift from grandparents or visitors.

As parents we have ample opportunities to teach our children that bringing someone into your home is itself a joy! The opportunity to share your family with a stranger should be a pleasure, much more so when the guest is a relative. To ask what the visitor has brought is demeaning at best and an insult at worst. Of course the child does not mean it, but it is as if he said, "The reason we anticipate your visits is because you bring gifts."

The grandparent who does not have the time or inclination to develop a creative or personal gift, such as the one given by my traveling friend, may consider purchasing a book for each child and reading aloud together. Reading a book is also an opportunity to give of yourself, and it says: "I want to give you a gift of ideas, not things. Toys and games are important and are the usual presents, but I, as a grandparent, want to imbue you with a sense of importance. I want to give you the world of thought."

In one way, a book represents this message.

10

LET HER STEW FOR A FEW DAYS

A good friend of mine owns a carpet store where I dropped in recently for a brief visit. I asked if he still enjoys the carpet business after all these years.

He said he does; however, over the last ten years he has noticed a drastic change in the way customers speak to him. Sometimes it is so distressing that he would much prefer that they do not even come into the store.

"Just a few days ago there was an irate

phone message on the answering machine. It was from a customer whose home I had carpeted three years ago. A metal carpet-strip had come loose, and the woman wanted me to come and fix it. Although the one-year guarantee had long since expired, I would gladly have come to repair it — if she had spoken to me in a pleasant, civil tone. Instead she was livid. She almost screamed into the phone, 'I insist that you – not your worker – but you personally come here immediately. Moreover, I will hold you personally responsible if anyone falls and gets hurt!'"

My friend became animated as he told me, "If she was trying to motivate me, she did just the opposite, because I let her stew for a few days. Eventually I sent someone to fix it, but I refuse to be intimidated by a customer. Even though I am just a lowly carpet man, I have enough self-respect to want to be spoken to nicely — and at this point in my business I can afford to lose an occasional customer who doesn't speak to me appropriately."

His words still reverberate in my ears: "If she was trying to motivate me, she did just the opposite."

We do things for one of two reasons: to gain something pleasant, good, or enjoyable; or to avoid something unpleasant, bad, unenjoyable.

While most people will respond to a demand which carries with it a threat ("If you do this, you get this...)" we must realize that unless we can, at the same time, make the process educational, we have really not initiated any change. As soon as the threat can be circumvented, the person will continue to do exactly what we have told him not to. We are treating the symptom, not the cause.

In dealing with young children, for example, it is our objective to introduce discipline and reinforce it until it becomes self-discipline.

Our hope is for the children to listen to us at first because they have to, but as they grow, they will begin to understand through our instruction why the positive behavior is desirable and accepted.

The time when grown-ups (or, for that matter, even children) can be forced or dominated is slowly disappearing.

While "dominating" children may have worked generations ago, for the most part, with exceptions, it does not work today. It may be effective with some children some of the time, but to believe that a parent can dominate a child is a mistake.

One of the basic themes that should permeate all *chinuch* is respect. Genuine respect will allow us to more effectively direct, teach, get responses, and have people listen to us. Many people "filter out" words and tones of domination. Commands such as "You must —," "You better do —," "I order you —," tend to bring out the worst in most people. Even in the most dynamic relationship, that of a *rebbi-talmid*, the Rambam writes that a *rebbi* should respect his student.

11

THE TIME BOX

Part One

or many years, every spring and every fall, we had difficulty explaining to our young children the "changing of the clock" from standard to daylight savings time, and then again from daylight back to standard.

I attempted to patiently explain about the twenty-four-hour clock and the fact that it was man who arbitrarily designated sunrise at 6 a.m., because it could just as easily have been designated at 5 a.m. or 7 a.m. — but it was all to no avail. Every spring the question was, "Where did the extra hour come from?" and every fall the question was, "Where did the extra hour go?"

In desperation, we created the Time Box. This was a stationery-sized box that was kept on a special high shelf in the basement and brought up with great fanfare on the *motzaei Shabbos* when the clock would be moved. Before the children went to bed, we brought up "the box," carefully took down the kitchen clock, and with a quick sleight of hand snatched the hour from the back of the clock and put it into the box! With appropriate ceremony I put the box on the basement shelf where it would reside untouched until fall, when we reversed the procedure.

Our little charade came to mind a few months ago when I saw a powerful visual demonstration in the teaching of time management.

The instructor brought a large box of household items and dumped them haphazardly on the table. The heap included books, cassettes, albums, plastic items, picnic utensils, notebooks, various articles of clothing, magazines, several partially full plastic bottles, and assorted household items. He then placed an attache case on the table and tried to fit all the articles into the suitcase. After he put just a few articles into the case, it was full. He put in a few more pieces, and it was crammed — and most of the items were still on the table!

It became obvious that there was no way everything would fit. So now he began to categorize the items based on what had to go, what could be condensed, what could be sent a different way, and what had to be left out.

For example, several utensils could be nestled together; a few pages of a book could be photocopied and the book left behind; the papers of several loose-leafs could be combined into one looseleaf binder; some clothing could be left at home; and the liquid from several plastic bottles could be poured into one bottle and the others thrown away.

He then separated all the items according to their importance and packed those which were most important *first*. Whatever space was left over he used for the next category, and so forth.

After we had an opportunity to absorb and

digest the concept of prioritizing, our instructor explained that time – the twenty-four hours of each day – has the same finite limitations as the suitcase. Just as there is a physical limit to how much matter can be put into a given space, there is a clearly defined limit to how much can be accomplished in one day! The challenge is to identify those areas that are most important to us, do them first, and then go on to the next item.

I once saw a statement that captures the essence of time management. In its simplicity it demystifies the time problem:

"Do a few things, the right things, one at a time, until completed."

12

THE TIME BOX

Part Two

One of our greatest challenges is to manage our time efficiently. It seems as if every new time-saving device – a second phone line, answering machine, call waiting, fax, cell phone, beeper, and e-mail – has instead further complicated our lives. Many of us find ourselves pulled apart by the different demands placed on us and the lack of time in which to do them.

You arrive at a *simchah* and see several people conducting business on their cell phones. You watch someone driving a car while listening to the chatter of a twenty-four-hour news station, attending to two children, and talking on the car phone, all at the same time. In addition to being rude and — in the case of a car phone — dangerous it is a *pizur hanefesh*, and that is what I want to address in these few lines.

Pizur hanefesh literally means "a scattered soul." This is the person who is trying to do two or more things at the same time, or whose feelings or emotions are pulling in opposite directions.

The peace of mind we would like to achieve is the opposite of *pizur hanefesh*. This is *menuchas hanefesh* – quiet, calm, peacefulness, a state of tranquility.

I had the privilege of knowing an elderly gentleman who trained himself to make peace of mind an art form. If he had a motto, it would have been similar to the one we previously mentioned: "Do one thing at a time, do it well, and complete it." When he came to shul to *daven*, his only purpose was to *daven*. Quite simple. The purpose was not to speak to anyone, not to catch up on the latest news, not to do anything but to come early, start at the very beginning, pace himself with the *baal tefillah*, say every word thoughtfully, and finish to the very end. If he did not talk in the middle of *davening*, it was not only because of the halachah involved, but because of the singular purpose at hand and his commitment not to do more than one thing at a time.

When he ate, he made sure that everything he needed was on the table, including *mayim acharonim* and a *Birchas Hamazon* booklet. He washed his hands, said *Hamotzi*, and ate his meal. He did not read while he ate and even refused to take a phone call — simply because he was eating.

I still remember the surprised look on the face of a young man who ran into this gentleman's home to get some financial documents and was told, "Not now, because I'm in the middle of eating, and I can't do two things at the same time." We may consider this an extreme measure, but the lesson is a powerful one. We may be able to adapt the basic concept to our lives in the following ways:

• When we speak to someone, we can give him our undivided attention.

• We can be especially careful not to interrupt someone who is speaking; and for that matter, we should not allow ourselves to be interrupted.

• We can train ourselves to take down phone messages carefully, noting who called, for whom, and the complete message.

• We can try to practice saying *berachos* and *bentching* slowly and deliberately.

• If we have to write a letter, do homework, or even read an article or a chapter of a book, we can set aside the ten or fifteen minutes that we need for the task and dedicate ourselves to the job at hand. With the exception of an emergency, we should not allow anything to distract us.

The purpose of these few suggestions is to help you develop an awareness of the value of dedication of thought. It may enable you to enjoy a new power of concentration that can lead to a significant measure of peace of mind.

13

ARE YOU LISTENING?

*A*n easy and effective way to show true respect for people is to listen when they speak. "Listen?" you may ask. "We constantly listen to other people." Yes, but...

I remember a parent who walked out of a principal's office with a look of total exasperation written all over his face. I innocently asked if anything was wrong, and he said, "Yes! I was at a meeting with the principal for over an hour, but I don't think he heard one word I had to say!"

That comment made me acutely aware of the different qualities of "listening." Over the years as I met with various people – principals, rabbis, executives, teachers, parents, businessmen – I carefully measured their "listening quotient." The basic measure I used was how many minutes of direct, eye-to-eye, uninterrupted attention I got. I found myself noticing how frequently and how intently these people really listened, and how often they allowed themselves to be distracted.

Let me describe two conversations at opposite extremes.

The first meeting was with an obviously overworked and overwhelmed executive in a small, crammed office. He cordially invited me in, pointed to a seat, and continued speaking on the phone as he read a letter. After he finished the phone call, he asked me to explain the purpose of my visit. My presentation (which I had outlined in a previous phone call and a letter) should have taken all of ten minutes, but before I even got started, we were interrupted by another phone call. During the next hour our meeting was disrupted six times by phone calls, twice by his secretary, and once by his co-worker who just walked in for a shmooze. Because this gentleman had so much work, his desk was piled high with unsorted papers. During the entire time I was there, he read several letters, signed them, made notes, and took care of several other pieces of business.

The unspoken message to me was, "You are unimportant to me. I will give you the least amount of my attention."

Before I was given an appointment for my meeting with the second executive, I had a phone conversation with him, and was asked to send in a summary of my presentation on a single sheet of paper. Then I was called and given an appointment for 4:20 p.m. and was told that I would be given fifteen minutes of uninterrupted time. I was asked to have all my facts and figures ready.

At precisely 4:20 p.m. I was ushered into the office as the executive said to his secretary, "My meeting with Mr. Shulman is important. Please hold all my calls, except for emergencies."

We sat down and within a few seconds he removed all the papers from his desk, set them on a shelf behind him, placed a new, lined yellow pad and his pen in front of him, and said, "I'm ready to listen!" And listen he did!

During the ten minutes of my presentation, he took an occasional note and asked a question to clarify a point. After I had finished, he said, "If I understood you correctly, here is what you said," and then read from his notes what I had offered to do for him and what he would be obligated to do for me.

After I agreed to his summary, he rose, shook my hand, and told me that I would hear from him in three days. Total time: fourteen minutes! Amount of one-to-one contact – 100 percent.

When I left his office, I was not certain whether or not he would accept my presentation — but I was certain that my presentation had had a full and fair hearing. This man paid me a tremendous compliment by the way he listened to me.

Not all of us can begin immediately to listen as intently as my second friend, but we can practice directing and focusing our attention on the people around us when they speak to us.

14

EREV SHABBOS DELIGHT

A full two hours before Shabbos her table is set, her kitchen is spotless, and she and her home are ready to receive the Shabbos Queen. She is fully dressed and now anticipating her special *mitzvah*.

She takes out her old, worn, blue loose-leaf address book and starts to make her *erev Shabbos* phone calls.

The story and motivation behind those

phone calls go back thirty years.

When she was a teenager, her father was stricken with an illness, and after several months in a hospital he passed away. The family went through the expected heartbreak, tears, loneliness, and financial difficulties. There were weeks and months that seemed to be totally bleak and black. However, each week there was one bright moment. Every *erev Shabbos* Mrs. Jacobs called and spoke to the girl's mother. Before her father's death Mrs. Jacobs had been a casual friend of the family, but somehow that changed. At the *shivah*, when hundreds of people came to offer their condolences and scores said, "Please call me if you need anything," Mrs. Jacobs had said very little. However, starting with the next *erev Shabbos*, after all the people had left, after all the expressions of sorrow had faded, Mrs. Jacobs had come over for just a few minutes. She said she knew how difficult this Shabbos would be and wanted to offer some words of support and some practical advice.

Afterward, every *erev Shabbos* just an hour or two before candle-lighting, Mrs. Jacobs would call. Most times the conversations with the young girl's mother lasted for just a few minutes − a few words of inspiration, the sharing of an uplifting thought, even a cute story. On occasion, when her mother needed to "talk to someone," the phone calls were lengthier.

There were two remarkable observations about the phone calls. First, they came *every* Friday. Regardless of how short the Friday was or where the family was traveling, Mrs. Jacobs always came through. Second, the girl's mother was always more upbeat, more zestful, and in a better frame of mind after speaking to Mrs. Jacobs. Even a three-minute call left her mother with a big smile.

Now, nearly thirty years later, the 16-year-old girl is a mature woman with a large family of her own. Her week is full, with a part-time job, car pools, homework, and community volunteer work. Yet every *erev Shabbos*, despite the pressures of her own preparation, she is determined to repay the *chesed* of Mrs. Jacobs. She has a list of sick, lonely, or forgotten people and calls them every *erev Shabbos*.

There is no great speech, no prepared copy, just a cheerful greeting, an expression of genuine interest, and an uplifting word. By keeping her calls relatively short, she is able to speak to ten to fifteen people in the one hour she allocates for this mitzvah. People have told her that her call is the high point of their week — and she fully understands that.

When she sits down to enjoy her Shabbos *seudah* surrounded by the smiling faces of her family, there is a special glow of satisfaction – you could call it *simchas hamitzvah*, the joy of having done a *mitzvah* – that she radiates.

In the middle of eating you may detect a soft smile when she thinks of a particular person who was touched by her call.

She knows the feeling because she has been there.

15

HOW TO
READ A BOOK

I recently read a statement that set me thinking: "There is little difference between someone who cannot read and someone who does not read."

Our age is called the Information Age. The number of books, magazines, and newspapers that are available is overwhelming. Yet, despite all the available reading material, few people have a systematic reading schedule. Most of us greet the arrival of a new book by glancing at the first few pages and then we put it away to read at a later time, a time which never comes. So we are left with a beautiful library of unread books.

I was taught how to read a book by a man who had a large library of books, all of which he had read, some many times over. These books were not just storehouses of ideas and information; they were also his best friends. He had a program to read several hours a week. He knew his books, and in his mind's eye had argued for and against their positions. As a result, he had developed his own ideas. When I asked him to share the one most potent idea on how to read, he suggested the following: Read with a pencil in hand. The objective of reading is to flood the mind with new ideas, information, concepts, and insights. Sometimes we can read ten pages or even one hundred pages looking for just one such idea, and when we do find it, we want to capture it and hold on to it.

The most effective way to capture and internalize an idea would be to write our new-found gem into a special learning journal. The physical act of writing reinforces the reading and helps us to remember it. As an aside, a learning journal is a wonderful concept on its own. It is a loose-leaf notebook in which we try to write whatever new thoughts we have learned that day. In a sense, it is a record of our personal growth. It allows and encourages us to review periodically how we grew in the last few weeks. It gives us a structure from which to project future growth.

If we do not write ideas down, the next best way to benefit from reading is to underline or highlight the sentence or paragraph in the book and/or to write in the margin of the page. The inside front-and-back cover sheets can also be used to list topics of interest and page numbers.

What we want is a method to highlight the key ideas so that they are readily available for reference.

We want to be able to go back to this book at some future date to review and locate the key thoughts, and perhaps find the one we are looking for, all in a short space of time.

As children we were taught not to write in a book because at a young age some children have the temptation to deface books. Obviously we are discussing underlining and note-taking done in an educational and dignified way, in a book that belongs to us.

I was once visiting a highly successful rabbi in a Midwestern community and asked him how he prepares his speeches. He pointed to a bookcase of biographies, history books, and storybooks and asked me to pick a book and to leaf through it. Nearly every page had underlined sentences, highlighted paragraphs, and marginal notes. He said, "If I read something interesting but can't find it when I need it, it isn't of any value to me!"

As I write these words, I am reminded of a very wise *talmid chacham* whose Shabbos table was always graced by a pile of *sefarim*. All had hundreds of notes, check marks, and other markings to call attention to interesting or important thoughts. When he opened a *sefer* to an underlined *vort*, it was as if the author of the *sefer* was sitting at the Shabbos table and had been asked to speak. The author came "alive" and joined his table. I can only imagine the rich heritage and the love of Torah thought he left to his family.

Whether or not you have the need to speak in public, we all have the need to be interesting people. An interesting rebbi or *morah* is a more effective teacher. An interesting parent is a more effective parent. Reading is one of the major ways we acquire new information necessary for growth. Developing more effective reading skills will enrich our lives.

16

IF IT AIN'T BROKE

wo relatively small incidents occurred in the last few weeks which carried an interesting message for me. I would like to share them with you.

I visited a friend early one morning, and he asked me to join him for a cup of coffee. I noticed a large plastic container of cornflakes on his kitchen table. On the counter were two more identical plastic containers filled with different dry cereals.

Knowing that my friend has a reputation

for creative and independent thought, I asked him why he had transferred the cereal from the cardboard boxes to the plastic containers. Instead of answering, he challenged me to think of some reasons of my own.

The first thought that came to my mind was storage efficiency. Cereal boxes are often much bigger than the contents, so why waste valuable shelf space?

The second reason I could think of was that the plastic containers kept the cereal fresh and protected it from infestation.

My friend acknowledged my answers and said both were correct; however, neither was the primary reason. "My main reason for taking the cereal out of the boxes was to take control of my breakfast table. I find the advertising, pictures, cartoons, and stories on the boxes to be garish and often silly. Why should my children and I have to stare at these tawdry advertisements? So we transfer the cereals into clear plastic containers!"

This reminded me of a time when I was at a friend's home for a Shabbos meal and noticed that he did not allow large plastic soda bottles to be brought to the Shabbos table. Instead, he had one of the children pour the soda into glasses in the kitchen and then bring them to the table. He told me that he had always been annoyed by these plastic bottles; but after seeing some monster bottles sporting the name "The Boss" and then, during the December holidays, realizing he had Xmas decorations on his Shabbos table, he decided that from then on he would be the boss and decide what would and what would not appear on his table.

The common denominator of both these incidents is the subtle lesson that it pays to think about ways to improve the quality of our lives (and, not so incidentally, the quality of our spiritual lives).

There is a well-known saying: "If it ain't broke, don't fix it." This implies that we should use our creative abilities only when something does not work. Obviously when something is broken, we need to replace or fix it. But we also want to improve situations that are working but could be made to work even better. While the two examples of the cereal boxes and soda bottles may seem insignificant, they do represent a challenge to improve any situation making it better, more pleasant, or more effective.

A student of mine used this idea to challenge himself to come up with ways of making his Shabbos table better – and developed a list of twenty ideas.

The key to this type of thought process is to believe that there are always better ways to do something. Even if we have been doing something a certain way for decades, there may be a way to do it better.

Once we are able to use this approach in almost any situation, we become open to better ways of living.

17

WHAT IS YOUR PARADIGM?

hat is a paradigm? This buzzword has become popular in the last ten years in management courses and seminars. Its definition is best described by a parable.

You have an important meeting with a client in Detroit. You fly into Detroit Metro Airport and call your client, who gives you directions to his office: "Take 94 East to 96 East and then go to Jefferson Avenue."

You buy a map and try to locate 94 East but you cannot. You look again but still cannot find it. You do find a small side street called East 94th Street many miles from the airport, but that does not make sense. You then search for 96 East and cannot locate that either. Regardless of how hard you look, you cannot find it – because in your haste you purchased a map of Atlanta rather than a map of Detroit.

If I asked you to define the difference between the two maps, you do not have to list the differences in streets, highways, or location of the airports. Rather, all you have to say is that one is a map of Detroit and the other is a map of Atlanta; then the hundreds of differences would all be self-understood.

The dictionary defines a paradigm as a pattern, example, or model. It is used to describe a vantage point or an outlook.

The thought occurred to me that this concept can also be used to describe two types of people. One person's paradigm is: "The world owes me." Just by being born, he is entitled; you ask, "Entitled to what?" "Not to anything specific – rather, just anything and everything!" Once a person develops a paradigm of entitlement, he has the right to demand from others. And he has the right to the "best" of everything. A popular commercial touts, "You deserve the best," as a matter to be taken for granted. This vantage point allows a person to be self-centered, to make sure he gets "it" first – and "it" is never enough. You can give this person a sizable gift, and his next question is, "When do I get more?"

There is a second paradigm which casts a totally different view on every aspect of life: "I deserve very little; in fact, what I do have is a *chesed* and gift from the Almighty. I am happy with what I have even while I strive to improve my situation."

You can see the sensitivity in the language. "May I please have" instead of "Give me"; "Do you think we should go there?" instead of "We're going there." This person has a relatively low expectation of what life owes him and is grateful for even a small gift.

In how many ways are these two people different? We can list scores of ways, or we can point to the one major difference: their paradigms of life.

The understanding of a "paradigm shift" becomes important when we try to improve our own behavior or to affect the behavior of a child. While it may be adequate to address a specific area — "I must begin a serious learning schedule" or "Chaim, please say thank you" — it is also important to keep in mind the possibility that perhaps it is the paradigm that has to be changed.

The story is told of a great rabbi who was asked, "What should the course of study be for a person who only has one half-hour each day to devote to Torah study? Should he learn *Chumash*, *Gemara*, or halachah?"

The wise rabbi answered, "Let him learn *mussar* for one half-hour each day. He will change his value system — and he will realize that he has more than a half-hour a day to learn Torah!" A beautiful example of a paradigm shift!

When we seek to improve, it may be to our advantage to be prepared, when necessary, to replace the map.

18

THE WALK HOME

The walk home from shul on Shabbos has to be of great interest to anyone involved in community life because it often mirrors the relationship between the rabbi and his congregants.

Imagine a common scenario. Because of a *simchah* there was an unusually large crowd, and the rabbi took the opportunity to discuss a thought on this week's *parashah* that he felt was relevant to a specific need. He may have spent quite some time in researching the commentaries on the *Chumash*, learning some *sifrei machshovah*, Jewish thought, and finalizing his presentation. He began his speech by asking an intriguing question, developed a beautiful thesis, quoted from *Chazal* to prove it, and finally brought home a moral and ethical point that could challenge existing behavior. Although the rabbi spent several hours in quiet thought, he was able to package and deliver the entire presentation in just nine minutes. The congregation davened *Mussaf*, wished each other *Gut Shabbos*, and walked home.

As the families are walking home, Moshe turns to Ben and asks, "Ben, what do you think of the rabbi's speech today?"

The next few minutes of conversation between Moshe and Ben can have far-reaching effects on them and their children beyond either of their imaginations. Let me tell you a story.

In a small *shtetel* in Europe in 1910, an 18-year-old girl announced that she was engaged to a local non-Jewish young man. She had had enough of Judaism and was ready to break away from religion, her family, and everything they stood for. Her parents were distraught. But pleading, begging, and threats did not move her one iota. Although her father had always ridiculed the local *rav*, in desperation he went to the *rav* and begged him to convince his daughter of her grievous mistake. The rabbi agreed. He spent an hour with the young woman, discussing many moral, ethical, historical, and religious issues that had a bearing on the situation — but unfortunately to no avail.

After the *rav's* unsuccessful effort, the angry father went to the town leaders, demanding that they fire the ineffective *rav*. The town leaders went to the *gadol hador*, who answered their question with the following story:

In a distant country, there was a doctor who discovered a cure for a rare illness that was fatal to young children. He went from city to city, and parents of children would come running to buy his miracle drug.

Late one night, the doctor was traveling by coach when a gang of robbers fell upon him, took all his valuables, threw his medicine into the river, and gave him a beating for good measure. He barely escaped with his life. The next day when he came to a new town, there was a long line of anxious parents waiting for him.

The first man in line, whose son was critically ill, begged the doctor for some magic medicine, and when he was told that all the medicines had been destroyed, he began to cry. "You were my last hope... and now there is nothing!" As he spoke, the doctor realized that this man was in fact one of the gang of robbers. When he confirmed this fact, the doctor said, "My friend, my medicine could have saved your son ... but it was you who threw it away!"

The *gadol* concluded by telling the committee of town leaders that if this man had honored the *rav* over the years, perhaps the *rav* could have saved his daughter. But he had always mocked and ridiculed the *rav*, and in a very real way he threw away the cure.

Now, listen to the conversation between Moishe and Ben. They may think that they are only discussing the rabbi's speech of this morning, but what they say, and especially how they say it, can have great impact. The truth is that children learn to value a rabbi, a *rebbi*, or a *morah* through the offhand comments of a parent or friend. It is these comments, not the official lectures he receives, which over time shape the children's opinions.

19

FLYING GEESE

There is an old joke in which Joe asks Moe, "Do you know why, when geese fly in a V-formation, one leg of the V is always longer than the other leg?" When Moe says he does not know and asks for the reason, Joe confidently answers: "Because there are more geese on one side!"

I do not know the reason there are more geese on one side, but I just came across some other fascinating facts about the flight of geese and the remarkable lessons we can learn from them.

1. As each goose flaps its wings, it creates a current of air for the other geese behind it. Thus, every goose following the leader needs less energy to fly and can increase its flying range by over 70 percent! Whenever a goose flies out of formation, it immediately feels the drag and hurries to get back into position. Perhaps we can learn from this to appreciate the value of common direction and a sense of purpose. Doing things in a group makes the task easier, more effective. Doing things alone means we feel the full force of the challenge.

2. The leading goose takes the full brunt of the wind. Leadership requires the ability to work hard and to do uncomfortable, unappreciated things. The leader has to know in advance that his job is tough and lonely, and that many times he will have to take action that is misunderstood at best and often unpopular. True leadership is doing what is right, not what is popular.

3. Because the leading goose gets the full force of the wind and has to work harder, other geese frequently rotate into the lead position. Similarly, we have to be sensitive to the

unusual pressures the leader is exposed to and try to compensate for them, at time alleviating him of the pressures.

4. The geese flying in the rear of the formation honk to encourage those up front, who have it tougher, to keep up their speed. Everyone needs encouragement, even leaders. The surprising fact is that even great people appreciate and thrive on the compliments of their followers.

There are many stories of truly important people who valued the compliments they received from relatively unknown people. A world-famous speaker, who would come to a small town and make a presentation, sometimes received letters from a local farmer, carpenter, or tradesman complimenting him on how well he spoke — and he would treasure those letters for years!

5. When a goose becomes ill or is wounded or falls out of formation, two geese immediately leave the formation and stay with the disabled goose until it revives or dies. Then they catch up to the original group or join another flock. The lesson here is obvious: the need to stand by our colleagues in difficult times.

The behavior of geese results from a built-in instinct. People, and only people, were given the gift to think, to change, to question, to improve.

We can find interesting lessons that have strong ethical and moral messages from simple everyday happenings.

As a parent and teacher, look for the opportunity to show a child an insight into something — how it works, why it is the way it is, and the lessons we can learn from it.

By pointing these out to the child in a casual, conversational tone, your message will not be intimidating and will have a greater chance of being heard and remembered.

20

KINDER WORDS

A young newlywed couple had planned on enjoying a pleasant dinner at a restaurant. After some conversation the wife suddenly raised her voice and indignantly said, "You're not listening to me!" The husband was startled and coldly responded, almost in a whisper, "I don't have to listen to you."

I suspect that the rest of the evening was not marked by the warmth they had both anticipated.

It took me some time to understand the subtle difference between "Listen to me!" – which the husband heard as a command: "You listen to me!" – and what the wife probably meant to say: "You may not have heard what I said."

Many people tend to downplay the difference between such phrases. They argue that the husband knew what the wife meant to say, so how important is it whether one word or another was used?

Yet words are the major way we express our thoughts, and since one person has no way to know what the other person is thinking, we really depend heavily on words. There are, of course, other ways to convey messages – tone of voice, gestures, body language. But in a large measure it is the choice of words that conveys our inner feelings.

Example: You call a friend and speak to his 10-year-old son, who informs you that his father is not home.

"Tell your father to call me," even with a "please" tucked in, is one type of message. "Please ask your father to call me" is a totally different one. A 10-year-old should not "tell" his father anything. He can ask or inform, but not tell. And I, the caller, would like to convey that message to him.

At a funeral I heard a man eulogize his former employer by saying, "I worked for him for over thirty years, yet I can never recall him ordering me to do anything. He would say, 'Harold, could you please do this?' or 'Harold, if you would be so kind and do this —,' but never, 'Do this!'"

What a nice compliment.

The effect is essentially the same; the employee understands that "Harold, could you please do this?" really means "I need this done," but the sensitivity to language makes it softer, gentler, easier to listen to.

If this is true of an employer–employee relationship, where a boss may be entitled to make demands, how much more so is it true in situations among friends or family.

I remember sitting at the supper table of a good friend and his family. His 8-year-old son, Shimon, had invited a classmate, Yaakov, home for supper. Twice, I had the opportunity to observe what, to me, was a phenomenon. When the father asked his son's classmate to pass something from the other side of the table, he said, "Yaakov, can you please pass the potatoes?" When he addressed his own son, it was, "Shimon, pass the vegetables!"

It is perhaps human nature that those to whom we are closest – our spouses, family, and co-workers – we take most for granted. The fact is that it is specifically to these people that our refined language and our thoughtfulness can mean the most. And the pleasant demeanor they exhibit as a result will make our lives more enjoyable.

21

VIDALIA ONIONS

*W*henever I suggest to parents that they utilize time spent at the supper table or during a car ride as an opportunity to speak with their children, I am asked, "Talk about what? School? The news? Politics?" I think the answer may be, "Talk about the exciting things happening in life." The Wall Street Journal recently had a story that I think is a perfect example of what can be food for an exciting family discussion. Following is a synopsis of the article.

Vidalia is a small town in Georgia. In reference to onions, however, Vidalia has come to mean twenty counties in the southeastern part of the state where the winter climate is mild and wet, and the soil has a low-sulfur content. Plant an ordinary Bermuda onion elsewhere, and it turns bitter, with an unpleasant aftertaste. However, in the special soil of southeast Georgia the same onion is juicy and sweet.

The humble Vidalia onion made it big in the late 1970's, when President Jimmy Carter, a native Georgian, started sending them as gifts. Today the Vidalia onion business is booming, with over 16,000 acres planted and onions selling at premium prices in gourmet shops and catalogs. The farmers are delighted!

But there is a problem. In every acre there can be a "hot spot" producing regular onions that are bitter and sour – not the type that can justify premium prices.

Enter Dovid Burrell, who, after two years of research, developed a device that could measure the sulfur content of an onion. He used this test in combination with the Global Positioning Satellite technology, which could divide a farmer's acreage into blocks of sixty square feet each. He could predict the sulfur content of the other onions within the block and relay the information to the farmer. The test worked! Two large growers signed for the exclusive right to sell "Certified Extra Sweet by Vidalia Labs, Inc." Articles about the testing appeared in trade publications, and soon buyers were demanding only tested onions. A few months later twenty-two growers sued both the inventors of the testing process and the two larger growers, claiming that their longtime clients were abandoning them in favor of tested onions and that they could not find a market for their onions.

Now to our supper-table discussion. First question: Who cares? It is a good question. All the growers, the inventor of the testing process, the investors, the supermarket buyers, the managers, even the local fruit-and vegetable-store owner − all of these people care. Ultimately, the price consumers will pay for Vidalia onions will be affected by the court case.

Now we can go a step further. Who is right and who is wrong? Can you argue one side of the suit? Can a child argue one side, and another child defend it?

What is the Torah viewpoint? The Mishnah in the fourth chapter of *Bava Metzia* discusses whether a storekeeper is allowed to give nuts to children to encourage them to continue buying in his store, or whether this is an unfair advantage over his competition. There are those who say it is not an unfair advantage because the other storekeepers can likewise give incentives. But what if the other merchant cannot compete? Can you deprive your competitors of their livelihood?

Can you envision an exciting, interesting discussion? All this from a lowly onion!

22

SUPPER TIME

I received an overwhelming response to the article about Vidalia onions. I wrote about a lawsuit involving onions and claimed that it was a good topic for an exciting family discussion. But what good could a conversation about onions possibly be? Allow me to address this now.

A *Rishon* asks the following question: Why is it that newborn animals leave their parents and newborn birds leave their nests and become totally independent in a relatively short while? By contrast, man, who is the most sophisticated of all creatures and the purpose of all creation, requires many years in his parents' home before he is capable of independent living. That is an interesting question. The answer given is that Hashem wants parents to convey *hashkafas hachaim* – the Torah's practical attitudes and behavior – to children, and this requires that the child spend years at his parents' side. If a child is to acquire and internalize his parents' way of thinking, their way of dealing with people, their way of preparing and observing Shabbos, and thousands of similar attitudes, many years are necessary. Therefore, Hashem created a system in which children develop slowly. It takes seventeen years or more before the child is mature enough to leave his parents' home.

We have now identified an important agenda in our relationship with our children. Obviously, we want our children to grow strong physically and mentally, to be learned and knowledgeable, to be *frum*, to be a "*mentch*." This is the dream and the prayer of every parent. We also want our children to absorb our life philosophy, especially in the area of *avodas Hashem* (serving the Almighty), both in direct service to

Hashem and in dealing with people. Especially in a culture where the Torah lifestyle is so severely challenged, we want our children to leave home with an immovable bedrock of belief and practice.

How do we convey our belief system to our children? The first response would be to teach them, to tell them, and to show them! And this is right. You have to teach, tell, and show them. But sometimes the direct approach does not work. Not all of us have the skills to teach, not every child always internalizes what he is told, and even "showing them" does not always do it.

I am suggesting that we also develop and nurture opportunities for open, nonconfrontational, and easy discussion.

To some parents, initiating such discussions may prove difficult, but it is a skill that can be developed. Like any new skill, it takes time, some experimenting, some disappointment, and some frustration, but if you keep at it you will eventually succeed. The results can be far reaching.

I would like to offer a few suggestions to make this process easier.

1. Do not sermonize. Let the *hashkafah* aspect

flow naturally. Do not be disappointed if, in the first attempts, there is no noticeable *hashkafah* development. Give it some time and eventually it will surface.

2. In real estate, the important thing is location, location, location. In developing open communication, the important thing is listen, listen, listen.

3. Reserve your own comments for last. Gently urge every child to make a contribution to the discussion. Be careful never to put down a silly comment, because you will thwart the process. The child who is put down may not want to make any comment next time.

There are many lessons we want to convey in our discussions. We want to say, "Life is full of interesting things if we just become aware of them." There is no actual separation between Torah which is learned in the *beis midrash* and life lived on Main Street or Wall Street. On the contrary, our Torah has a practical viewpoint on every aspect of life.

In addition to nurturing the body, the supper table can afford an opportunity to nurture the mind and the soul.

23

GUILT

What do you teach your children about guilt? Is it good or bad? In order to understand guilt, let us use an analogy. Guilt can be seen as a correlative of pain.

Physical pain such as a toothache or stomachache is a physical message saying, "Something here is in trouble. Correct the problem." Touch a hot stove or prick your finger with a needle, and the resulting pain indicates present danger.

If it were possible, would you want to eliminate this type of pain? Not unless you would be content to allow a small, easily remedied cavity to go unnoticed until the tooth abscessed, an infection to go untreated until it disabled an organ, or your body to suffer serious injury before you became aware of the danger. Understood in this light, pain is a friend, a valuable warning system, a gift from the Almighty. The intelligent response to pain is to identify its cause and rectify the problem. Once this is done, given appropriate healing time, the pain should subside and disappear. It has fulfilled its mission. If, once the cause of pain has been corrected, the person were to seek ways to maintain or prolong the pain, we would consider this a psychological problem.

Guilt is the pain of the soul. It flares its head when you have violated your own value system. As an example, a person believes that stealing is wrong, yet he was tempted to steal and gave in to his temptation. As a result, his actions are out of balance with his beliefs. Just as a needle invades the nerve endings in the finger and signals that something is wrong, the violation of a person's value system is signaled in the form of guilt. Once we identify and correct the problem by going through the process of *teshuvah*, the feeling of guilt has served its intended purpose and should subside.

The Almighty created man unique in his ability to change. Whereas every other creation is set on an unalterable track – a cow cannot decide to give chocolate milk, an apple tree cannot provide pears – man alone can voluntarily elevate or lower his value system, at the point at which guilt is triggered.

For example, the person who previously believed that stealing was wrong begins to associate with gangsters and then joins a gang which robs and steals. By stealing numerous times, he effectively lowers his own value system to the point where stealing no longer causes guilt. His new, lowered guilt threshold may lead to worse violations, such as harming or killing his victims.

Similarly, a person can elevate his value system to the point where he believes that fooling a person, "stealing" his time, or waking a person and stealing his sleep is wrong. By associating with righteous people, by reading inspiring stories, and by studying ethical behavior, he can develop new beliefs. When he internalizes these new beliefs, they will become part of his upgraded value system and send him signals if he violates them.

This is a fascinating thought. By focusing his attention and carefully selecting the material he feeds his mind, a person can adjust his own values and corresponding guilt threshold! We are thus challenged to improve and refine our values.

Is guilt good or is it bad? The answer is yes; it is both good and bad. When used as intended, to warn us of a problem, guilt, like pain, is good. This is very good, because it allows us to rectify a minor problem before it becomes a major one. After we have corrected the problem, if we still wallow in guilt, it becomes negative and self-defeating.

The Almighty created man to function physically, emotionally, and mentally in balance and in harmony. It is up to us to use, not misuse or abuse, either body or soul.

24

THE TELEPHONE

Part One

hazal tell us that a good measure of a person's character is how he handles alcohol, how he spends his money, and how he acts when he is angry.

In contemporary life there are two other minor but interesting areas which test our behavior. One of these is how we use the telephone; the other is how we drive, which we will discuss elsewhere in this book.

I remember reading a story about a farmer who, after lengthy deliberation, had a party-line telephone installed in his home. For our younger readers, a party line was an economical phone line shared by four families at the time when telephones were first installed. Families would know by the number of rings for whom the call was intended.

A few weeks after the phone was installed, the farmer was eating supper when a neighbor came over to visit. As they were talking, the phone began to ring. The farmer ignored it. It rang again and again, but the farmer continued to eat, totally ignoring the phone. Finally the neighbor said, "Joe, isn't that your ring? Why don't you answer it?" Joe looked up and said, "Yes, it is my ring, but I had the phone installed for my convenience. Now it ain't convenient!"

If we were asked to find a word to describe the phone, we might use indispensable or essential, but not convenient. For most of us the phone changed long ago from a convenient tool to one that is disruptive and often annoying.

In Chapter 26 we will discuss how to keep the phone available for emergencies without allowing it to control us. But here we will be dicussing the ordinary, everyday use of the phone.

If we want to control our use of the phone, here are a few concepts to consider:

1. A ringing phone does not always have to be answered. For example, during supper or family time, we do not have to accept any calls. On occasion I have called a friend and have been informed either by an answering machine or in person, "Our family is eating supper. May I ask you to call back in an hour or may I give my father a message to call you?"

The power of this choice came across to me several years ago when I was invited to eat supper at the home of a good friend. Before washing, he removed the receiver from the phone and said to me, "You know, the next forty-five minutes are the most important part of my day because I get to spend them with my family — and they are the most important people in my life. I don't want to be interrupted by a phone call!"

The family then began their meal, during which they discussed varied and interesting subjects. Every child sat through the entire meal, even the younger ones who barely understood the discussion. It was as if the whole outside world was on hold. The only thing that was happening was the family.

After *bentching* the father put the receiver back on the phone, and once again the household was plunged back into the world.

2. Teach your children how to answer a phone properly. The most effective way to teach this is to do so yourself. When you answer a phone politely, with a smile and a warm greeting, it can change the disposition of the caller. Moreover, it may qualify as a fulfillment of *Chazal's* instruction: "Greet everyone with a pleasant disposition." This is especially meaningful if you do not know who the caller is!

3. Teach children how to summon someone to the phone. Very often a child answers the phone, and then, in an ear-piercing scream (that you can almost hear without the phone), shrieks, "Chana, it's for you!!" That message to Chana is that there is a call for her; the message to the caller might be that the house is a zoo.

25

THE TELEPHONE

Part Two

n the previous chapter we discussed two aspects of the telephone. The first was to designate family time when calls would not be accepted, the second was to answer a phone politely and warmly. I would like to continue our discussion. Here are some further ideas for productive and meaningful use of the telephone:

4. The telephone gives us an opportunity to teach our children how to take messages. Taking a message patiently, fully, and care-

fully is a mark of maturity. The cost in time and aggravation caused by incorrect messages – appointments missed, meetings changed – is staggering. In addition, not promoting the proper way to take a message contributes to an attitude of sloppiness that may have far-reaching consequences. To make message-taking easier, provide a message board or notepad.

5. Teach children how to leave a message. A message has meaning when it includes the time of the call, the name of the caller, the person for whom the call is intended, a call-back number, and, when appropriate, the purpose of the call. Since answering machines and voice mail have become accepted ways to communicate, it is even more important to leave clear and complete messages. When you come home from a two-day trip and find eighteen messages on your machine, you quickly learn to appreciate those that have all the necessary elements and a recognizable call-back number.

6. When calling, consider the time of day and be sensitive to the happenings at the house you are calling. For instance, it is not a good idea to call a mother at supper time or late at night. I have been asked important

career-related questions, that require discussion and thought, at inappropriate times. How much more thoughtful and effective it would have been if the caller had asked, "I have an important subject to discuss; is this a good time for you?"

7. This brings us to call-waiting. I once called a friend who said at the beginning of our conversation, "Yes, I do mind." He explained that often, the person to whom he is talking gets a call-waiting click and says, "I hope you don't mind," and clicks off, without even giving my friend the courtesy of three seconds to answer! So he has decided to tell people at the outset of a conversation, "I do mind."

Increasingly I find that people hang up when they are put on hold for another call. Their reason: "If you're talking to me, for goodness' sake, talk to me." Obviously there are exceptions, such as when you are expecting a doctor's call; in such cases, inform the person at the beginning of the call.

8. Cell-phone etiquette is another important area of discussion. The cell phone has removed conversation from the privacy of a home or office and placed it out in the public

arena. I have occasionally been embarrassed to overhear people's private lives being discussed openly, often loudly, on a cell phone. We have seen people using a cell phone in shul, at a *shiur*, at a wedding, in a bus, on the street, and in restaurants. The cell phone also allows anyone to interrupt you even in the midst of a deep conversation with an important person. Anyone who has your number can call, and our curiosity about who is calling us often supersedes our better judgment.

I think every family, for its own sake, must establish boundaries of proper and poor taste in the use of a cell phone, and decide when and how a cell phone should be used for business and social calls. Can you justify using a cell phone when it is possible or probable that you will disturb those around you? And even if you do not mind spreading your personal concerns around, perhaps there are people nearby who would consider this an imposition.

The availability of a phone allows us to stay in touch with friends, do *chesed*, encourage people, learn (we know parents who continue their nightly learning with their children even when traveling). Torah Umesorah's Partners-in-Torah and the Daf Yomi are great examples of using the phone for *mitzvos*. But the availability of a phone also invites negative usage, even tempting us to waste our time in meaningless talk.

Speech is the Almighty's great gift to man. We must use it properly, taking care not to allow the advancements of technology to control our lives. We still have choices; we have to learn to exercise them with greater care.

26

EMERGENCIES

*I*n the previous two chapters we discussed phone etiquette, limiting the use of the phone, and other aspects designed to free us from our enslavement to this device. However, we neglected one important area: how to keep the phone available for emergencies without allowing it to control us.

I would like to use this idea to address an even broader topic: how to keep one relatively small obstacle from coloring our attitude toward an entire situation. Here is a relevant example, which also involves the problem of being available for emergencies.

I once gave a time-management workshop to a group of principals, administrators, and teachers. As soon as I began, I realized that the principals, almost to a man, had an impenetrable mental block and were very resistant to the ideas I presented. I asked one of them to explain this to me, and he said, "Since we have to be available at all times for emergencies, few time-management ideas could possibly apply to us!"

I had just presented the idea of blocking out an hour and a half every second day for some quiet thinking and planning when I was met with a clamor of responses: "I have an open-door policy and have to be available all the time"; "I can't disappear for an hour and a half because I have to be available for emergencies."

I asked my friends to draw up a list of what they considered emergencies. The answers included a child being hurt, a teacher having to leave the classroom, an unexpected visit from a member of the Board of Education, a family member becoming ill, a call from the bank regarding an overdrawn account, a call from the president of the School Board. When we had a list of ten examples and thought we had covered every contingency, I pressed my participants for two more "emergency" situations. Now that we had a completely comprehensive list, I asked, "How often do any of these things actually happen each day, week, or month?" The answers ranged from one to five times a week. I then suggested that they give the list to the secretary with the following instructions: "If anything on this list – or anything remotely similar – happens, please interrupt me immediately. But if it is not on the list, please tell the caller that I will return the call later in the day."

I was gratified by the way the principals accepted this suggestion. But even more gratifying was the fact that once the mental block of the pressure to be available for emergencies was put into the proper perspective, they were open to other new ideas.

The purpose of this particular chapter is not to discuss time management, but rather, as we have mentioned, to discuss the idea that we often allow 1 or 2 percent of a situation to color our attitude toward the entire situation. Many of us do this in different ways:

• The homemaker who does not have the self-confidence to make one particular dish, and therefore does not invite guests to her home.

• The young man who has great ideas, but because he is poor at spelling is afraid to commit his ideas to writing.

• The person who is computer illiterate and is afraid to apply for an interview even in a field unrelated to computer use.

• The person who does not have an adequate understanding of a subject and is afraid to go to a *shiur* because it will be over his head.

• The person who refuses to speak in public because he is afraid of mispronouncing a word.

• The teacher who refuses to consider any new discipline ideas because he keeps thinking about the one student for whom they will never work.

We have a tendency to allow the 1 or 2 percent – the areas in which we are doubtful or insecure — to force us to set aside the remaining 98 or 99 percent! We develop a philosophy which says, "I can't do it because — Therefore, I won't even try to think around the problem." We allow these minor obstacles to paralyze our thinking process to such an extent that we are convinced we cannot overcome them, so why even waste time thinking about it?

Life experience says that when a group of intelligent people sit down with an open, positive attitude to solve problems, unbelievable results can and often do happen.

If we are willing to consider setting aside the "2 percent," unexpected and refreshing new possibilities will likely happen.

Now let us go back to our original problem of the phone. If you have aged parents or children and are concerned about emergencies, here are three ways that you can keep the phone line open in case of need without allowing it to disrupt your life:

1. Install another line and give the phone number only to those about whom you are concerned. This will allow you to disengage your home phone during supper and still have peace of mind.

2. Purchase an inexpensive beeper which would be used only for emergencies.

3. Use a telephone-answering machine which would monitor who is calling. A family

member can listen to the calls as they come in, and in the event of an emergency, answer the call immediately.

I hope I have made two points clear. The first, really minor point is about maintaining control of our telephone usage. The second and major point is about challenging our thought processes. Dismissing a new suggestion or way of thinking simply by saying, "It can't work for me because..." is often an easy way out of solving problems.

27

COPING

Part One

*L*ife has never been easier than it is in our time, and yet humankind has never seemed so fundamentally out of sorts.

We can buy whatever we want without cash. Our clothes, food, and amusements all come ready-made. We can speak instantaneously to anyone in the world, on impulse. The mere turn of a dial will customize the temperature of our air, wash dishes, do laundry, or blow leaves from our well-manicured lawns. It has been estimated that the average home has electrical appliances that do the work of more than thirty servants.

At the same time that we are taking such good care of ourselves, all the indicators of social decrepitude — violent crime, moral nihilism, drug and alcohol abuse, family distress — have soared beyond our worst imagining. How can we interpret the fact that the historical period of greatest personal ease is characterized by the greatest incidence of personal discontent ever known to man?

One does not have to look hard to see a causal relationship at work here. Just consider the frame of reference we have created for ourselves in the lap of this industrialized, affluent society. A culture which teaches that effort and discomfort are to be avoided at all cost, that waiting is a waste of time, and that "no" is a terrible word is a culture which prevents us from acquiring the coping skills of life. Steadfastness in the face of difficulty, patience for the sake of long-term rewards, self-discipline — these are abilities which allow us to cope, and no one can achieve a lasting happiness without them. But where, in the raising of today's children, is the training ground for these vital abilities?

Do we really want our children to inculcate contemporary mores? Don't we want something more for them — the ability to have meaningful, unassailable family relationships, the qualities of steadfastness, patience, and self-discipline, the ability to say "no" to destructive cravings?

If contemporary culture is fostering in today's generation the inability to cope, we as parents have an obligation to teach our children how to deal with the painful contingencies of life. We cannot give a child almost everything he wants, teach him to shun difficulty, and then expect him to grow into a mature human being. Where will he learn the first lesson of maturity — to delay his need for immediate gratification? Or the second — to have staying power in a relationship? Such vital lessons cannot be taught overnight. They require a sustained and comprehensive effort on the part of the parents. They are the work of a lifetime.

Coping — dealing ably with difficulty — is a skill that can be taught like anything else. It needs to be demonstrated, practiced, and reinforced over time. A child raised in a religious home has the best chance of succeeding as a mature adult because he will have been raised in a framework which encourages en-during values and which trains him to control his instincts for the sake of a higher good.

We will give you information about six cop-ing mechanisms that you yourself can use and which you can pass on to your children.

28

COPING

Part Two

Every parent wants to prepare his child for dealing with the temptations he is certain to encounter — and the pitfalls he may very well succumb to without proper training. Given today's cultural values, building strength of character and emotional maturity in our children requires a comprehensive program of moral training in the home. A few strategies consistently applied throughout a child's developmental years will help him to achieve true maturity as an adult. Here are the six tools we promised you earlier:

1. Teach your child how to do for himself. A toddler starts learning how to get dressed at the moment his mother hands him his own shirt and pants. Trial and error teach patience, as well as helping a child focus on a long-term goal.

2. Provide the child with a repertory of deeper values. If you want your child to become a loving, caring adult who is capable of meaningful relationships, he will need to feel that life has enduring, transcendent meaning. Talk alone is not enough here, since the evidence your child will confront in the world is stacked against you. Your life has to reflect these values in real terms. This is one reason religious family life typically is stable.

3. Say "no." Do not be afraid of the word — and do not feel guilty about saying it. A child thrives on structure, and it is your job as a parent to provide clear ground rules for him to follow. "No" is the first step in teaching your child to cope. Once he can accept "no," he begins to learn how to accept adversity, how to delay gratification of a desire, and how to deny himself inappropriate temptations.

4. Support the child at difficult moments. Explain to him that learning can be uncomfortable, that many of the great rewards of life come only with effort and patience, etc. Help him to devise appropriate solutions to his problems — and encourage him to talk about them. This will help to defuse many of the frustrations of growing up.

5. Provide positive reinforcement. Rewarding a child for an act of maturity — self-discipline, patience, or the ability to manage a difficult situation — will take the "sting" out of a lesson learned. This reinforcement will also reward him nicely for a brief period of delayed gratification.

6. Be a model. Children are beings with the distinct inability to delay their desires, and today's social mores only reinforce that inability. A child needs to witness coping in action. He needs to have an alternative frame of reference established in his mind as a positive value. The more ably you and members of your family deal with difficult situations, the more likely your child will too — in the long run.

Not even a master teacher or experienced parent can teach coping skills as a subject. A child who suspects he is being lectured to will tune out, and you will have lost the game in the first move. But living a Torah life-style with joy and passion, creating an atmosphere of purpose and delight, will encourage your child to learn these skills in a positive way. Watching you repeatedly forestall your own gratification for the sake of performing a *mitzvah* is a superior lesson in character-building; and the framework of enduring values which *Yiddishkeit* provides is the surest counter to the empty cultural values that will almost certainly, at some stage of his life, entice him.

29

HOMEWORK

Part One

*F*ew demands promote the discord between parents and children that homework does. In no other area of education does the school infiltrate into the home, involve parents, and position parents and children against each other. Yet homework fulfills a vital educational need.

The irony is that if you were to ask principals, teachers, parents, and students why homework is given, you would probably receive many different answers.

Why homework?

The answer that comes to my mind is that homework in the younger grades is designed for review, and in the older grades also enables the student to prepare for forthcoming class work. Since there are only a limited number of class hours a week for each subject, assigning work to be done at home frees valuable class time for teaching and discussion – activities that require a group dynamic – and relegates those activities that can be done individually – reading, research, report writing, reviewing – to nonclass time. As a child progresses through school, the ratio of class time to private learning time changes dramatically to reflect the shift from "being taught" to "learning." In the primary grades, the ratio may be five or six hours of class time to one or two hours of homework. In high school, it might be five to three, and in higher education it might very well be two or three hours of class time to ten to fifteen hours of private time.

For educators, the homework ratio is a message: In addition to teaching text material, the main objective of school is to give the student the ability and tools to think on his own and to engender in him a love of learning. Just as the objective of parental discipline is to teach the child self-discipline, the purpose of teaching is to develop a student who eventually becomes a self-sufficient, self-educating adult. The purpose of formal education is to produce young men and women who will continue to learn for the rest of their lives. It is a foundation leading toward learning in its totality.

It has been said that, unfortunately, many people today subscribe to the Vaccination Theory of Education: Learn enough about the subject to make sure that you never go further.

As Jews, the idea of learning for a higher goal is self-evident. We view learning Torah not only as a means of acquiring the knowledge to do *mitzvos*, but also as a unique obligation and a way to get closer to the Almighty. While all *mitzvos* are important, the *mitzvah* of learning Torah is the spiritual catalyst that provides the impetus to properly perform all the other *mitzvos*. It empowers the Jew's day, week, Shabbos, and Yom Tov. It vitalizes his private, public, and business domain. It guides his every relationship. Learning Torah gives added meaning to every *mitzvah* and becomes the spiritual and emotional bedrock that provides a person with stability and clarity in a changing and often confusing world.

When education — both religious and secular — is viewed in this light, work to be done by oneself at home takes on an entirely new meaning. Contrary to what students often think, the purpose of homework is not to vent the teacher's frustration. It is — or should be — the real preparation for a mature and meaningful life.

It has been said that homework can be a great equalizer. To a child who is having difficulty in class, homework holds out an opportunity to catch up to his classmates. Equally important, it offers him the chance to internalize the truism that almost anyone can learn anything when he is willing to invest the necessary time and effort.

30

HOMEWORK

Part Two

When a teacher gives a lesson, the top third of the class may immediately understand it; the middle third may partially understand it; and children in the bottom third may leave with varying amounts of knowledge and confusion. Rather than allowing him to give up, having a child work at home, at his own pace, so that he can succeed, reinforces his belief that sometimes it may take him longer to learn something, but given time and effort he can learn it and do it well.

Can you imagine the difference it can make in a child's self-esteem when he has learned year after year to meet the challenges of work and activities that do not come easily? Can you visualize the far-reaching impact that his belief in himself can have on his future? Studies by the California Assessment Program reaffirm what common sense tells us, namely, that homework helps raise test grades. Tests done in California show that seventh-grade students who consistently did two hours of homework a night scored 20 percent higher than those who did not do homework.

THE WORD "HOMEWORK" IS A MISNOMER

The word "homework" means work that was assigned by a teacher to be done at home. Since not every teacher assigns homework nightly and the parents must rely on the child knowing what the assignment is, the parents are at a disadvantage. A child can easily say, "We don't have any homework today." However, the parent does not have to think in terms of "homework." Instead, he or she can initiate the concept of "study time" or "reading time," time that is set aside after school for independent activity. The study time can be used to read, write, organize thoughts, prepare for future assignments, or read supportive material. The idea is that each student needs time for himself to balance schoolwork. While younger children will need constant help in their study time, as they grow older they will do more on their own.

The parent may want to prepare a variety of interesting reading material and activities so that there will always be something to do during the study time. A trip to the library and a selection of newspaper and magazine articles (Jewish, of course!) can stock a corner full of exciting materials.

In an article I read, parents are encouraged to help their children keep a homework log. Ask the child to record each day's assignment and show it to you. Go over the list with the child before he begins his study period. The log will not only make clear what is to be done, but will also emphasize the importance and value that you place on independent work.

THE PARENTS' ROLE

The parents should carefully walk the tightrope between support and challenge. On one hand, if you do the work for the child, even if he learns the material, you are defeating a major intent of the homework assignment:

self-study. On the other hand, you do not want to see the child overwhelmed by work that he cannot master. Perhaps a few minutes of clarifying an underlying principle or cutting through a misunderstanding will help. But if you actually do the assignment, you are learning the lesson, not your child.

INSIST ON A DISTRACTION-FREE ENVIRONMENT

No lasting learning can take place when a radio is blaring, friends are talking, and the telephone is constantly ringing. The parent should make it clear that proper study requires full concentration. In fact, the nonverbal message here is that whatever you do should be given your full attention and full effort. Sharing your attention and inviting distractions means at the outset that you are agreeing to do less than your best.

HOMEWORK IS PREPARATION FOR LIFE WORK

Homework — or, better stated, self-study — is really preparation for good, lifelong study habits, and these habits can make a tremendous difference in the quality of a child's life.

31

GRANDPARENTS

D o you remember your grandparents? And if you do, of what do your memories consist?

Every once in a while you meet someone who tells you how his grandfather or grandmother enriched his life. He will relate a special relationship that he had with this grandparent, and how, decades later, lessons his zeide or bubby taught him are still vividly alive in his mind.

How varied are the stories that come to

mind. There is one of a grandfather who every Friday would review the weekly *parashah* with his grandson. Those two hours each week became an eternal bond between them. To this day, decades later, every time this man (who is himself a grandfather) reviews the *parashah*, he remembers how his grandfather explained a *Rashi*, or told him a *midrash*.

Another cherished story is of a mother of a large family who, as a young girl, would go to her grandmother's home to help cook and bake for Yom Tov. The recipes, the aroma, the joy of doing a *mitzvah* together, and the casual conversation did not only become vivid memories, but were also woven into the fabric of this woman's personality. Many times today she can hear herself saying to her children — verbatim — a comment that her grandmother had made to her many years earlier.

Today, for the most part, grandparents are younger, more active, and more fully involved in their own lives. Often they live in a different city, if not in a different country than their families.

Question: Given that society and life-style differ from that of previous generations, what is the ideal role of Jewish grandparents today? Usually, the grandparent will come to visit occasionally, bring presents, and acknowledge birthdays. But my question goes beyond this. In which ways will or can grandparents enrich and enhance a grandchild's life, making a lasting contribution to the child's personality, one that will bear fruits for decades?

I do not have enough answers that satisfy me, and I look to others to offer their suggestions. In asking this question, the following two ideas were suggested, and they represent the kind of answers I am seeking. Easy to do, inexpensive, and simple.

1. A well-known *Rav* would pen a birthday letter to each grandchild. The parents saved these letters in a loose-leaf folder, and the child would accumulate these letters in addition to Yom Tov and special occasion letters. The letter written to a 3-or-4 year-old may be a simple, one-line greeting. As the child grows, each new birthday letter by its tone and content acknowledges the child's progress and advancement. Can you imagine the treasure these letters became in later years!

2. This idea comes from a grandmother who lives in America and is frustrated by not be-

ing able to be part of her grandchildren's growing-up process in Eretz Yisrael. In addition to her occasional visits and three minute phone calls, she sought a way to bond with the young children. Her solution: she purchases inexpensive children's books suited to the grandchild's age, reads them aloud into a cassette player, and sends the book and cassette to Israel. In this way, the grandchild can hear Bubby reading a story while following the pictures and text.

Making cassettes offers a tremendous opportunity for maintaining closeness, but many people are afraid or uncomfortable with the recording process. By reading a book on a cassette you will overcome this fear and find yourself speaking freely about other things as well.

To our readers: Do you have any ideas or suggestions on how to bond with grandchildren, especially those in a distant city? I would greatly appreciate hearing from you.

32

RETIRED?

A friend's father who lives in Boston underwent an operation and I inquired about his welfare. In the conversation I asked what his father did. "My father is retired. He spends the winter in Miami, the summers in a bungalow in the mountains, and doesn't do much else." My face must have registered a surprised look, because my friend realized that I had expected more of an answer, and as an afterthought added, "My father is also a great Red Sox fan, and he avidly watches all their games."

Assuming that at some point a person's major financial obligations are taken care of, and his children are on their own, the question now becomes, what does he do?

This is the time of life that society has held out to us as the "golden years," the time when we are free to do what we truly want to do, instead of what we have to do. The ads have depicted these years as the time to fish, travel, indulge in the sport of your choice, play golf, and to generally enjoy life. After all, these ads point out, you "have made it" through the most difficult years of raising children and the perils of earning a living. In addition, in the Jewish community, we have survived tuition committees, Bar Mitzvahs, *shidduchim*, our children's career decisions, and now we have earned the right to the good life! I have no qualms with the concept that the "golden years" entitle a person to a well-deserved respite from the pressures of the daily grind. But after the respite, the question still becomes, "Now what?"

There are those who have bought into the idea that pleasure and enjoyment as a way of life are acceptable or even desirable. To them, this question (and this chapter) will have little meaning.

But to those of us who have spent our productive years giving, doing, building and growing, will the daily retirement schedule of pleasure and enjoyment be enough?

There is one additional observation: Age is a technical function of the clock and calendar. "Growing old" is, however, a concept usually described by words such as: used-up, spent, stale, decrepit, and retired.

The fact is that there are men and women well into their 70's, 80's and 90's who are vibrant, exciting, fresh, and enthusiastic about life.

What would you imagine to be a major factor as to why one person is old and spent, and another is vibrant and enthusiastic?

Surprisingly, health, family, and financial independence are relatively minor factors. The major difference is: Does this person have an overriding reason to live, a purpose to achieve?

Studies made by insurance companies verify what our own observations indicate; namely, people who at age 65 retire, only to relax and enjoy, live fewer years compared to those who throw themselves into a major project.

This brings us to another interesting point. How real are the "dreams" so many of us have? You hear people saying, "When I retire, I will —" It could be a materialistic dream — travel, fishing, golf — or a spiritual aspiration; to learn, do *chesed*, etc. We all know people who all their lives assured us (and themselves) that when they will have the time, then they will become *bnei yeshivah* ... then they will learn two full *sedarim* (sessions) a day, etc. Yet, when retirement finally does come, they find themselves unable to fulfill their dreams!

This idea is expressed in the following short sentence:

If you are not now actively involved in getting what you want, you really do not want it enough.

A test of how you might use your retirement time for a planned project is how much time you devote to it while you are still gainfully employed.

You will be surprised as to how many people fool themselves for years with the words, "When I have time, I will —"

33

A NEW PHENOMENON

*I*n many Jewish communities, seeds of a revolution are evident. The numbers are still small, but a perceptive eye can discern a trend.

I am speaking about the phenomenon of *baalei batim* who have become earnest Talmud students. It may be a doctor who learns in a *beis midrash* in the morning and opens his office at 12:30, an entrepreneur who learns from 4 o'clock to 7 o'clock every evening, or a retired businessman who has "joined the *kollel*." In almost every *beis Medrish* you will find successful people who, although they may never have had the opportunity to learn in their youth, have decided in later life to become *bnei Torah*.

Perhaps it is the ripple effect of the popularity of the *daf yomi*, the publication of the ArtScroll Schottenstein Talmud, the availability of cassette and telephone *shiurim*, or the affluence of the population. The facts are that there are scores of men who are taking learning *Gemara* very seriously.

I believe that as people mature, there is a realization that they are lacking something both important and enjoyable. They are deficient in spirituality. When we are able to still the hustle and bustle of our daily life — when we can shut off the intrusion of phones, beepers, and e-mail; when we can set aside our pursuit of business successes; when we can shut down the incessant clamor of the media, when we can tone down the influence of friends and community — intelligent people ask, "So is this all there is?" *Mussar sefarim* state that one of the most effective ways that the *yetzer hara* has to keep us from recognizing the truth is to keep us so busy, occupying our minds so fully, that we will never have time to consider where we are going. Has there ever been a time in history when there have been more opportunities for our minds to be kept occupied? In the past, even when people worked ten and twelve hours a day, when they were not working, they had time to think! Today we have surrounded ourselves with tools of communication: phones, radios, computers, internet, cell phones, to insure that every waking moment our minds will be engaged. We have almost no time to think! In view of the *baalei mussar* quoted above, this gives the *yetzer hara* the upper hand.

There is one more contributing factor as to why mature adults are choosing to learn. That is the *Baal Teshuvah* movement. Walk into Ohr Somayach or any other yeshivah geared to late starters and you will realize that these yeshivos are populated by intelligent, wholesome, successful young men and women who are prepared to change their lifestyles, friends, value systems, and sometimes, even their careers, because they have found a new joy in learning Torah!

The *Baal Teshuvah* movement — in addition to what it has done for these men and women — says to all of us it is never too late to learn!

Once a person gets even a small taste of the "*geshmak*", the joy, of learning, he can easily get hooked. Learn a page of *Gemara* in a class, review it seriously with a *chavrusa* (learning partner), ask a good question, and find that the commentaries ask that very same question — and they provided brilliant answers, which, because you asked the question, you fully understand — and you say to yourself, "Wow! This is pure joy."

Imagine walking along an eight-foot-high fence that surrounds a construction site. You hear bulldozers, machines, men at work, but because of the fence you cannot really see anything. All of a sudden, you come upon a tiny six-inch window. In one sweeping glance, you get a picture of what is happening. You do not know much about the building, but you did get a glimpse. You now know what the machines are doing. You have a vague idea of what it is all about. In the same way, we see *talmidei Chachamim* who are 50, 55, 60, even 65 years old, learning intently, for twelve hours a day with tremendous enjoyment. We see it and ask ourselves, "Where is the joy? What keeps these people so occupied, motivated, and satisfied?" Then we, too, embark upon our journey in learning and acquire just a teeny taste of a good *kasha* and *teretz* (question and answer), and we have a small window into the joy of learning.

In our community there was a man who began to learn at age 65 and at the time of his death had completed *Shas* two and a half times! He would review the *daf* several times a day.

To all of us the message is clear – it's never too late — so let's begin.

34

CREATIVITY

Part One

What is your attitude when confronted with a problem? Do you view it as a challenge and attempt perhaps to find a solution, or do you give up?

With creative thinking one can often solve challenges even in areas outside of one's area of expertise.

Here is an example of how imaginative thinking can solve problems:

The first challenge deals with a narrow

bridge leading to an island. The bridge is just wide enough to allow for two-way traffic. However, to enable some repair work to be done to the bridge, the double roadway had to be rerouted into a single lane.

Problem: This is the only bridge to the island. It must be available to the one hundred island homeowners to allow them to travel in both directions. Since one cannot see the traffic coming from the opposite direction from either side of the bridge ramp, how do you control the traffic to avoid a head-on collision?

We have all encountered flagmen who stand on the end of the construction road, allowing traffic to go in one direction, and then by hand or radio signal change the direction of the traffic flow to the opposite direction. But how do you do this for several weeks in a place which is used twenty-four hours a day?

This problem was solved by the use of portable "traffic lights." A traffic light (or "red light" as we call them) was placed on a trailer, with an arm suspending the light over the roadway. Two trailers were used, each one placed on an entrance ramp to the bridge. The device sent a radio signal to change the light from red to green, so that for one minute the southern entrance would be red and the northern entrance green. The next minute the process would be reversed. Power for the traffic light came from sunlight, but could just as readily be from a gasoline generator. Simple?

The idea is not even unique because the use of traffic lights to control traffic is surely nothing new. (In fact, it is the oldest, safest, simplest method of traffic control!) What is unique is applying an existing idea in a different way to solve a new problem.

We mistakenly think of creativity as a special gift that belongs to an elite group of inventors and scientists (usually characters) who are holed up in a garage or laboratory "inventing things."

The truth is that as children we all possess the gift of creativity to some degree. To a large extent, it is the pressure to conform, albeit necessary, first at school, and then in society, that stifles our creative impulses.

Studies show that although young children have a heightened degree of creativity, as they mature it is lost. What a shame! The ability to creatively solve problems can enhance a person's life at all times, and it becomes especially important in the face of crisis.

The ability to cope with an unpleasant or difficult situation goes hand in hand with the person's core belief that he has the ability to discover a solution to a problem. There are many children who are never encouraged to think creatively, but are rather led to believe, "That's the way it is and we can't do anything about it." This attitude smothers them and they may find themselves unable to handle even mild rejection, such as being left out of a group activity or losing a class election. They will surely be unprepared for life's major crises such as the loss of employment, illness, etc.

Creativity begins with the basic belief that we are able to put on our thinking caps and thereby solve problems.

35

CREATIVITY

Part Two

*I*n the previous chapter we discussed step one of creativity: to believe that we can solve problems. The example we discussed was controlling two-way traffic over a one-lane bridge, with the use of portable traffic lights.

Here is another interesting example: A large supermarket is built, with the parking lot located on the roof.

Problem: Customers do their shopping on

the ground level, fill their shopping cart, and then need to take them to their cars. How can we provide a method of getting them to the roof without the use of an elevator?

I'll try my best to describe the solution that was employed. We will start with a motorized walkway. (Many airports have flat walkways to move people, luggage, and carts from one terminal to another.) The walkway used in the supermarket is a long incline going from the ground floor to the roof.

The challenge is how to put a shopping cart full of food on this inclined walkway so it will be secure, will not shift sideways, will not roll back down, and will still be easy to get on and off the moving walkway.

We usually think of a brake as a device that either presses against the wheel so that it can-not move (as in a bicycle or car wheel), or locks the wheel so it can not roll (as in a hospital bed, projector table, or wheelchair). What would happen if we placed the wheels in a groove so that they would spin freely while the cart itself would rest on small immovable feet? The ability for the cart to roll on the wheels depends on the wheels touching a surface. But when the wheels do not touch a surface but are in a groove, they cannot roll. Moreover, the wheels locked into the groove will prevent the cart from moving sideways. By using a grooved rubber surface we solved one part of the problem.

The next challenge: How do we prevent the shopping cart from rolling back, as it goes up the incline? The solution is ingenious.

Next to each wheel of the shopping cart is a small piece of metal — a 3-inch foot with a rubber tip. When the shopping cart is on level floor, the "foot" rides a quarter of an inch above the floor; it clears the floor. When the shopping cart is on the rubber walkway, the wheels fit into the groove and the small "feet" now touch surface. The cart no longer is resting on wheels, but rather on its feet.

The rubber tip at the bottom of each foot is wedged against the walkway and resists the backward motion of the shopping cart, just as a doorstop is wedged against the floor and resists the closing door.

The result? A shopping cart, riding uphill, locked into place.

As the walkway comes to the top, it gently nudges the shopping cart on to the flat floor. The wheels again make contact with the floor, lifting the cart to its normal position. The small feet again clear the floor, and the shopping cart rolls easily.

This method has been in use for the past year with thousands of people using it daily. It is simple, safe, and easy. Interestingly most of us are familiar with the components of the solution; the grooved walkway and the small feet with rubber tips. The creativity is to bring these together in a new way.

Previously we suggested that the first rule in teaching creativity is to believe that by using our heads we can solve problems.

The next step would be for a teacher or parent to challenge the children to use creativity in solving problems. When the adult wants to encourage inventive solutions to problems, why not ask, "How would you solve this problem?" Listen carefully to the answer; without evaluating it. Do not say, "Of course it would not work for these obvious reasons," but ask rather, "What else can you think of?" Listen to four, five, even ten ideas, and you will be pleasantly surprised at some of the ideas which will be concocted.

At that moment, whether or not a child does come up with the right answer is really not important. What is important is your teaching them to not be afraid to think "out of the box."

If you can then show them an actual solution someone else devised to solve the problem, you will have made the lesson complete.

This could be a fun activity and meaningful exercise, with a highly serious message.

36

DRIVING

Part One

*D*epending on where you live, work, shop, and where your children attend school, driving a car has become an integral part of our daily activity. To many of us, learning how to drive a car, finally passing an official driving test, and getting a real driver's license is a "rite of passage!" It is the moment when instead of "having to be taken," we can drive ourselves! It really means we are grown up enough to be trusted with "life";

which in this case means returning the car in an unscratched condition. Equally important, it says to us that we can go wherever we want to! (Ask any 16-year-old to explain this to you!) However, the first blush of independence slowly wears off and driving becomes a task. This is especially true for the commuting adult who may also have to ferry several children in a car pool.

In the following chapters I would like to make several specific comments concerning driving, but at this point I just want to share a few general observations.

1. When teaching his children to drive, a friend of mine always begins with the following rules: Rule #1: *You never drive when you cannot see!* After the snickering and giggling stops, he explains that there are many situations when we cannot see the road ahead such as when we go over a hill, around a curve, around a bus, truck, or even a car, in a fog, at night (if we outpace the beams of our headlights), going in reverse, sitting on a low seat or behind a covered windshield, driving with glare from the sun or strong lights in our eyes. It really does not matter why there is reduced visibility and you cannot see. The rule is simple; you do not rely on assumptions,

if you cannot see, you do not drive. Over the years I have come to realize that this wise rule really applies to many additional situations in life, business, careers, investments, friendships, etc. When it is an important matter, do not rely on assumptions. To avoid mishaps we have to actually see what lies ahead.

Rule #2: Regardless of the road surface: asphalt, cement, dirt, ground, ice, snow, wet leaves; regardless of the weather: sunny, clear, rainy, snowy, windy; regardless of traffic: heavy, light, or nonexistent; regardless of the light condition: daytime, nighttime, dusk, dawn, fog, *you must always keep both hands on the steering wheel!*

Driving means having control, and in a car, having control means holding the steering wheel.

It would be foolish to think that even if we had perfect weather, a clear beautiful highway and no traffic, we would be safer or have better control by not holding the wheel. Yet, as ludicrous as this may seem, there are people who argue that since there is no way we can fully protect ourselves (there is always the possibility of an oncoming drunken driver), it makes little difference if they hold the steering wheel (take full control) or if they do not.

We all know of people who drove cars in excellent mechanical condition, new tires, perfect alignment, good brakes, etc., yet they still had an accident. These two facts may be true, but they do not change the dictates of common sense: When you control what you can control, you increase the chances of a safe trip.

Consider these points in driving a car, but realize the analogy to many other life's situations in life.

How often are situations allowed to occur and continue without being taken under control? They reason — incorrectly — that since they can not control the entire situation, why bother to take control at all! The lesson learned from driving cars should be clear: You must always be in control of that which you can control!

Rule #3: Imagine someone driving at 80 miles per hour. He is pulled over by a state trooper. In attempting to explain why he was going so fast, he says, "Officer, it really was not me who was speeding; it was my car that was speeding; because my accelerator is set on cruise control." The truth is so obvious it needs no explanation! The one who sets the controls is the one who can change them, and therefore is the one who is responsible. This is, indeed, basic and elementary.

Think about that the next time you hear someone else (or yourself) say, "That's the way it is," or "I always do it that way and I can't change." True, many habits and attitudes are on "cruise control," but since he can always change them, since he can change the settings, he is responsible. This is an interesting thought.

37

DRIVING

Part Two

riving a car is a true exercise of our *middos* (ethical behavior) for two reasons. First, it tests our tolerance to frustration under adverse conditions at the worst time. Second, it frequently sets up a confrontation with others. Yet, just because of these difficulties, the way we drive a car can become a learning opportunity for our children in many areas of life. The beauty of this realization is that there is no need to lecture, or to criticize anyone. The lessons — some of them major lifelong lessons — can be taught so subtly that children will hardly realize they are being taught anything. It is teaching in its highest form — modeling behavior.

Driving a car bring you into situations where you interact with others. You may own a home or apartment, but not until someone comes to your door and wants to come in do you have the opportunity to exercise your rights as owner. But every time you get into your car, act and react in traffic, and attempt to park, there is a constant seesaw balance between your needs and rights versus the needs and rights of every other driver and pedestrian.

The simple act of pulling out of your driveway into the street puts you up against the cars coming down the street. Do you first let the cars pass you, then pull out; or do you first pull out, even though it will cause the other drivers to slow down and even to stop? Whose rights and needs have priority?

The use of a horn is likewise a good example. Originally invented to alert a pedestrian or oncoming car of impending danger, the use of the horn has expanded to include the heralding of arrival! When we go to pick up someone, as soon as the car comes within earshot of the person's home, we begin to honk the horn. Never mind that the sound of the horn disturbs the tranquility of a neighborhood, and possibly annoys the neighbors. "It's my car, my horn, and I can use it as I please." If we were to suggest that the driver wait for a moment, that the person being picked up be ready at the appointed time, that the driver use his car phone to call the person to come out, or the far-fetched idea that the driver actually get out of the car and go to the door, our suggestions would be considered impositions. The needs of the driver (to conveniently inform the person that he is waiting) and the needs of the neighbor (peace and quiet) are in conflict. Whose rights and needs come first?

Let us discuss traffic. Let us assume that a 40-mile trip with no traffic may take less than an hour; with moderate traffic, one hour and fifteen minutes; and with heavy traffic one and a half to one and three-quarter hours.

You may remember that years ago, that same trip in heavy traffic took only one hour. You may have even "done it" in one hour in the middle of the night. But, the facts are that at this time, with traffic, it will take longer. No matter how angry you get about it, regardless how you may rant and rave about the traffic, it will still take you one and a half-hours to drive the distance.

The *Gemara* in *Kiddushin* has a pithy saying: Bar Kappara says, "An angry person comes away with nothing but anger." The only accomplishment of anger is that you remain angry. This simply means that your anger will not change anything, except make everyone around you upset.

The newly coined phrase, "road rage," accurately describes the disposition of many drivers as they try to beat the traffic. But ask yourself: Do you intentionally want to put yourself into a position of rage when you could have avoided it by setting out earlier? Do you want to teach your children how to get into a rage, with all its undesirable side effects, when some planning could make the same trip more enjoyable?

Talking about coming late and blaming it on traffic brings us to another point.

Calmly arriving twenty minutes late to an important meeting with the excuse, "There was a lot of traffic," is not really acceptable. Coming late sends many messages. One is: "My time is more important than your time and I have no problem making you wait."

Leaving at the last minute or not taking normal traffic conditions into account (with the exception of something truly unusual) is really a statement that says, "I don't know how to gauge situations," or worse, "I can't manage my affairs properly." Or the message might be: "I don't care if I arrive late." Whichever, blaming traffic is a lame excuse.

38

DRIVING
Part Three

We discussed how driving pits the driver's needs against the need of others, and how important it is to take into account that "traffic delay" is a given.

Here are some additional observations:

- I once read that 90 percent of all accidents at intersections happen within the first ten seconds after the light changes from red to green. If we train ourselves not to dart out in the first few seconds, we can appreciably decrease the chances for such accidents.

This brings us to "patience." I know that the time from school to home, home to school, car pool to shopping is measured in microseconds. However, test after test shows that by cutting all the corners — being first out at the light, constantly changing lanes, using back alleys, etc. — the driver has gained a negligible amount of time. But the tension, anger, and rage acquired is considerable.

- The anonymity of a car on the highway allows for an interesting display of character. When a driver is cut off or when someone takes a parking space he had waited for, a person who is generally well mannered, and even mild mannered, has been known to become a changed person. He uses unbecoming or even profane language because a) he feels he is 100 percent right and b) the other driver does not hear him so he is really just venting his frustration.

- Have you ever been in a car when the driver was cut off and then goes out of his way to show the other driver who is boss? The fact that one person is right hardly justifies the danger to the passengers of both cars. Then there is the revenge aspect. Imagine the lesson conveyed to children if when the parent's car is cut off the child says, "Let's get him, Daddy," and the father calmly answers, "No, that's not how we live. His wrong doesn't justify my doing wrong."

- What is our attitude toward all the laws of the road? Every child's eye is keenly watching to see if 65 miles per hour means 65, or 70, 75, or 80 (with appropriate excuses). When I hear people bragging about how fast they drove, it always makes me wonder what they are teaching their children.

- Parking has its own set of rules, depending on where you live. In some communities you are "allowed" to make a late *Minchah* by double-parking for ten minutes, blocking another car. Such behavior is often righteously excused by pointing out, "It's a *mitzvah!*" and then shrugging, "He won't mind." All *mitzvos bein adom l'chaveiro* (*mitzvos* between people) require time, effort, and sometimes expense. Parking a car where it is permissible and will not interfere with anyone is no different.

I discussed these concepts with a friend who asked me, "If the Chafetz Chaim were alive today, what would he say about driving?" I did not want to even offer a suggestion, but my friend said, "Perhaps the Chafetz

Chaim might say: 'Drive safely and drive in a way to make a *Kiddush Hashem.*'"

Driving safely would be no less than the fulfillment of a direct *mitzvah* of the Torah to take special, extra care of our safety and welfare.

Driving in a way to make a *Kiddush Hashem* opens new vistas of opportunities into the driving experience. Imagine not sounding a horn at the first second of a light change, allowing another driver to go ahead of you, allowing a pedestrian to cross a street unhurriedly, or driving within the speed limit. These are no longer expressions of weakness or being a "*neb*" — on the contrary, they are ways of making a *Kiddush Hashem.* What a qualitatively better way to drive on the highway of life!

39

DRIVING

Part Four

I n this chapter I would like to focus on the positive opportunities that driving has to offer.

One of the reasons why we are so frustrated by driving, especially those who regularly commute by car, is that we view "driving time" as unproductive. We think that we could or should be doing so many other important things, and here we are stuck in traffic or just driving. This frustration causes us to utilize every short cut to arrive at our destination — to do something. We take unnecessary risks although we are aware that our safety is being jeopardized.

Perhaps one or more of the following ideas can make driving time more productive, and thus more enjoyable.

1. Private time. In a day crammed with things to do, phones that never stop ringing, people to speak to, and meetings to attend, we can find little private time for ourselves. Yet, we all need and can greatly benefit from time to think, digest, allow ideas to gel, and enable us to get in touch with our own thoughts and feelings. As important as the opinions of others are, we want to build into our day quiet time to do our own thinking.

If we can change our paradigm from viewing our commute as "how quickly can I get from point A to point B," to the idea of "how can I use my commute time as quiet, private thinking time," it would open new opportunities. This new way of thinking may mean perceiving our forty-minute drive as a fifty-minute drive; it may mean going a different route (the scenic route) or it may mean leaving earlier or later. The objective should be to capture the commute time for ourselves — not empty radio, tape or cell-phone time, but quiet thinking time.

2. If we can incorporate some of the ideas listed above, we may want to view the commute time as a great opportunity to relax. Perhaps enjoyable music would help. But in order to relax, we have to drive nonaggressively, and be willing to allow for the extra few minutes.

The father or mother who comes home after a relaxed drive is a totally different person than the person who, after a day of business pressures, drives home with "road rage." Whether he realizes it or not, his children may want to hide from him until he calms down and rejoins the human race.

3. There are thousands of cassettes covering every conceivable topic that can make driving time enjoyable. You can hear an interesting thought, listen to an inspiring story, or even indulge in some "light" learning. Obviously, we are assuming that listening to these cassettes will not distract you from driving safely.

Several years ago a friend of mine became a commuter, and began listening to Torah cassettes available on loan at the local library. Within a short period of time he has heard hundreds covering a wide variety of topics by world-class lecturers. He told me that his commuting time had opened a whole new world of thought for him, a world he would never have known, and which he thoroughly enjoys.

Do not be fooled into thinking that cassettes are only for those who have lengthy commutes. You will be surprised at how quickly you will finish listening to a 60-minute cassette while doing local errands. Until you actually time it, you have no idea how many minutes you spend in a car for your day-to-day needs.

4. Because of all the distractions in our homes and offices, there are times that a car ride is a wonderful opportunity to really talk to someone without interuption. If the traffic is not a distraction (again that depends on one's frame of reference, more so than the actual flow of cars), you can find an hour-long discussion in the privacy of a car to be a most rewarding experience.

40

DRIVING

Part Five

*D*riving plays such a large role in our lives that I have devoted five chapters to it. In this chapter, I want to discuss three more facets.

A family trip can be an enjoyable way of spending quality time, or a nightmare of endless bickering, where the question, "Are we there yet?" is always in evidence.

The difference between the two will depend, as with so many other things in life, on the amount of planning you are prepared to invest in this project. Depending on the age and number of children, appropriate games and stories can be prepared. As the children grow older, you may want to assign each child a half-hour which is his to fill with a story, speech, play, song, or game. You may be interested to know that there are several books written just on this subject, and you can probably find them in your local library. I saw a series of cassettes in which the narrator gave the history of local areas. The cassettes were meant to be played as you drive along a specific stretch of Route 95 and are pegged to the various mile-posts. How about older children preparing some history of the areas along the road you are traveling?

An interminable drive can become a time to allow each child to have center stage for a while. In a large family, there are often one or two children who almost never have that opportunity; the car ride can become a sought-after time for them.

Usually a family traveling between two cities does not have the time to consider a detour, but you may find that the extra time involved will make the whole trip much more pleasant. I know of families that traveled hundreds of miles, stopping several times for an hour or two, transforming a difficult trip to one that the children thoroughly enjoyed.

Family car trips can become children's richest memories. They will long cherish the family togetherness, the meals, the singing, and the new places they visited.

The opportunity to act appropriately and do *mitzvos* on the road — *Tefillas Haderech, berachos* before and after eating, *davening,* learning — even where to go and what to see — all become guidelines for our children on how to behave away from our usual surroundings. It pays to invest time and effort into planning such a trip.

How to plan a trip can in itself be an interesting insight into your own thinking.

Many people get into a car and just go. They have a general idea of the direction and a great deal of confidence in their sense of direction. They will tell you, "There are road signs, and we will find it!" We are all for a positive attitude, but even a great positive attitude is no substitute for knowing exactly how to get where you want to go.

There is an art even to such a simple thing

as getting directions. I was once in a rural area, and when I asked a local farmer for directions, he just said, "Make a right at the next traffic light." It was only after I drove twenty-one miles to the next traffic light did I realize I should have asked him, "How far is the next traffic light?"

Get accurate directions from a knowledgeable person (ask how far you have to go on each road, and what landmarks will help you identify each turn), verify the instructions with up-to-date maps, and write the directions in large print on a pad so you will be able to read them as you drive.

One last point. The condition of the inside of the car says a lot about the driver. I am sure you have been in cars whose seats are piled high with old paper bags, empty soda cans, banana peels, maps, books, clothing, and an assortment of other things. There is usually an embarrassed apology, something about the children and a recent trip with no time available to clean up.

Whereas you may get some warning before someone comes into your home, you usually do not have that luxury before someone enters your car. Your car is an extension of your home, your office, and your own room. You will feel so much better in a neat and orderly vehicle and so will everyone around you.

41

A GOOD FIGHT

One of the exciting things about learning Torah is that you may learn the very same concept ten times, and when you learn it again for the eleventh time, you discover a brand new thought, a gem of an insight that you never noticed before.

There is a fascinating Rashi in the story of Korach that can teach us much about ourselves.

When Korach and his group challenged Moshe Rabbeinu, the Torah relates that Moshe said, "In the morning Hashem will make known the one who is His own, and [who is] the holy one." Rashi comments, "Why next morning? Because now is a time of *shikrus* (drunkenness), and it is improper to appear before Him."

The question is: Who is drunk, and where does intoxication come into this discussion? There are those who learn that Korach and his group had eaten their main meal of the day, which was usually accompanied by wine. *Sifsei Chachamim* comments that they were involved in dissension all day, and therefore Moshe Rabbeinu said, "It is a time of drunkenness." We find that the word "drunk" is sometimes used in this way — "drunk, but not from wine." Rashi used the word *shikur*, drunk, to describe a condition that usually is a result of ingesting alcohol, but in this situation was the result of daylong fighting.

The effect of alcohol on the mind is fascinating. When one drinks several ounces of alcohol, he can no longer think clearly and loses his ability to understand and to control the body. A person who is drunk does things that are ludicrous, foolish, and demeaning. The fact that alcohol intake results in intoxication is a given. Although the amount of alcohol necessary to diminish control may vary depending on body weight and other factors, the basic rule is the same: When you imbibe alcohol, you are not in control. Just as there are physical laws such as gravity, which are absolute, so too there are laws of human dynamics that are universal.

Imagine a person saying that because he is good, rich, special, learned or kind, the laws of gravity or alcohol do not apply to him. It makes little difference who he is; the physical law applies universally.

Rashi is teaching us, by the use of one word, a powerful equation — an insight into our behavior. Just as the effects of *alcohol* physically cloud the mind's functioning, *fighting* clouds its functioning as well.

The practical lesson to us is clear. A person should know in advance that when he gets involved in a heated argument, he will lose his ability to think clearly.

We have seen people do inappropriate things in a confrontation; acts that are irrational, foolish, demeaning actions which are harmful to themselves and to their loved ones. When we ask, "Where is your common sense? Where is your discretion?" we are never given an adequate response.

Rashi is defining this behavior with the use of the word "drunk." Can you reason with a person who is drunk? Can you ask him, "Where is your common sense?" Obviously not. In the same way, once a person has become involved in a fight, he risks losing all common sense.

What a beautiful insight into our holy Torah; what a rich understanding of ourselves.

42

WHISPER POWER

Many years ago I read a story that remained in my memory for decades. It was about a family of six robust boys, ages 4 to 14. Every morning the mother took her position in the kitchen like a sergeant and began barking orders: "Jack, sit down! Murray, leave your brother alone. Eli, start eating your breakfast," and so on. This continued through breakfast, cleanup time, and getting ready for the school bus. When she finally put the last child on the bus, the mother dragged herself into the house, went up to her bedroom, and collapsed.

She developed a throat problem and, after a doctor's examination, was given some unpleasant news. She required a minor procedure and then total rest for her vocal cords for three months!

The procedure went smoothly. On the way home from the hospital, it occurred to this woman that for the next twelve weeks she could not be in charge of her morning command post. The problem gnawed at her: If her children barely made it to the school bus *with* her screaming and yelling at full force, what chance was there for her to control them without her voice?

The story then described how she learned to give instructions by pointing and smiling, and to convey a message with a glance or a flick of the wrist. The calm that resulted was so appreciated by all her children that they asked her to continue in the "quiet mode" even after her vocal cords returned to normal.

Years later she looked back at that medical procedure as a turning point in the running of her home and in her relationship with her children. She wrote that not only did the children respond more readily to her quiet approach, she was not burned out by the time the children boarded the bus.

I have a friend who is the principal of a large high school. When he has to admonish a student he has the student come to his office and wait there for a considerable amount of time. The student is then invited into his office, expecting to be yelled at. Instead, the principal sits at his desk, and begins to whisper to the student. The student can hardly hear him and has to lean forward to catch each word. The few sentences spoken in this way earn 100 percent attention because the student is really listening.

Compare that to the scenario where a parent, teacher, or principal yells. As soon as the decibel level goes up, the average student blocks out the message.

Obviously there are times when yelling is acceptable, even desirable. It is necessary when conveying a message of impending physical danger, for example. But when yelling is a way of life, it loses its effectiveness.

Yelling as a way of getting someone to do

something is degrading. Try whispering and speaking softly. The *pasuk*, "The words of the wise are heard when spoken softly," will work for everyone.

AN APPRECIATION OF RABBI DOV GREENBAUM זצ"ל

How will one remember Rabbi Greenbaum? Obviously each person and every family has to answer this question individually and differently: the wonderful son, the devoted husband, the father whose greatest pride was seeing his children become *talmidei chachamim*, the grandfather whose joy was watching his grandchildren learn, the concerned brother and family member — each of these facets can be recorded so much better by others. I would like to share my thoughts on the mechanech facet of the Rabbi's life.

First and foremost, I would like to remember the Rabbi as a *baal ruach*, an individual with a driving, positive, moving spirit who was bold enough to dream big — very big — and practical enough to personally attend to the details of these very same dreams and bring them to fruition.

The Rabbi was that rare individual who could, in the span of just two hours, make a passionate plea to a group of parents to become involved in a yeshivah fund-raising activity, go on to thrill a roomful of bar mitzvah guests with an uplifting Torah thought, move on to test and inspire an eighth grade class, and still have the time and patience to guide a new teacher on the technical details involved in writing effective worksheets.

The man who could challenge and provoke a county official when he acted contrary to the interest of the Jewish community was the same man who was moved to deep emotion by just the mention of his beloved Eretz Yisrael. The person whose impromptu speech to a group of sixth graders as they began a science lesson was a classic presentation of deep Jewish thought was the same man whose spirit would soar to hear a *berachah* recited by a bright-eyed 3-year-old.

The Rabbi was a superb teacher — master *mechanech* — who could enter into any class without prior preparation and capture the imagination of each student with his knowledge and presentation. He was a person who was supersensitive to the highest form of education — personal example:

The *talmid* who finishes many *masechtase* on Mishnayos today does so — perhaps unwittingly — because the Rabbi encouraged, motivated, and energized this project!

The young boy or girl who *davens* well today does so — perhaps unknowingly — to a large extent because the Rabbi, in his own life, set high standards for *tefillah*.

The *beis medrash* boy who learns well does so — perhaps without realizing it — because the Rabbi, with his own genuine love for learning, set the tone for *hasmadah*.

The man or woman whose life centers around a *tzedakah* or a *mosad* does so because of the personal example set by the Rabbi.

The older *baal habayis* who even today enjoys learning at a *shiur* does so because of the inspiration and *geshmak* projected at *shiurim* the Rabbi magnanimously delivered for over *thirty* years!

And the couple who exhibit a meaningful love for Eretz Yisrael, and move there years later, do so perhaps unaware that this love for Eretz Yisrael is the outcome of overflowing love that the Rabbi felt and taught.

The immediate Yeshiva of Spring Valley family — the *rebbis*, teachers, office staff, and students — were permeated by the personality and dreams of this one man. When the yeshivah was still just six classrooms in an old building situated on the Old Nyack Turnpike in Spring Valley, the Rabbi was already dreaming of a modern edifice to house and educate 350 children safely and with dignity. When the yeshivah had 250 children in one building in Monsey, the Rabbi was already dreaming of a two-building complex in which 700 boys and girls could learn Torah with great pride.

The Gemara teaches us that one of the attributes of a *talmid chacham* is to be, when necessary, unyielding, tenacious, and strong — and what strength the Rabbi had!

Strength to confront anyone — parent, contributor, community member —

who challenged a Torah value. Strength to stand up to the moneyed interests of a shopping center planned for the corner of Rte. 306 and Maple Avenue. Strength to proudly and defiantly stand for an unpopular position because it represented a forward movement for the yeshivah. Twenty-five years ago when every yeshivah in America ended its school year in June, the Rabbi saw the acute need for Torah summer classes and had the strength of conviction to fight for it and convince *rebbis*, parents, and students — and set a trend which many would follow.

And the same Gemara likewise teaches us that the very same *talmid chacham* should be, when necessary, soft, yielding, and compassionate — and how tender and feeling the Rabbi was! How many late evenings — after a long day of yeshivah business — or Friday afternoon, just a few minutes before Shabbos, was the Rabbi involved in a *chesed* to which he could not or, more accurately stated, did not want to say "No!" How many personal hours did he take away from his cherished Gemara and his beloved family to help someone because, in this situation, at this moment, the *mitzvah* was to be compassionate.

Allow me to share several highlights that stand out in my memory:

1961 — The Rabbi was guiding a new teacher. "There are two ways one can teach a child how to make a *berachah*. A loving father will use the opportunity of giving a child a piece of candy to teach a *berachah*. An unthinking camp counselor will use the opportunity of loud thunder — when the child is frightened and hiding under the bed — to teach the child the *berachah* to be recited when hearing thunder. Teach with love, teach with your heart."

1962 — We were watching cement being poured for the foundation of the new yeshivah building when I asked the Rabbi, "How can you construct a building when the yeshivah is eight weeks behind in payroll?" The answer was simple and pointed: "Never be afraid to go ahead."

1965 —   A Purim play was hastily prepared and required participation of the Rabbi. We hesitated to ask the Rabbi to "act as himself" in the play. "Rabbi, is it befitting for you to do this?" The answer, "If I can serve Hashem and the yeshivah by acting in a Purim play, then it is befitting."

1968 —   The Rabbi had just challenged the Board of Directors to purchase a property at a cost of $96,000 when the yeshivah did not have the $500 necessary toward the down payment! The Rabbi's answer to the obvious question, "Have *bitachon.* The children need it. We will get it."

1971 —   At an Executive Committee meeting one very late night, all six of us were desperately trying to convince the Rabbi that now was the wrong time to start a building campaign. His answer, "Nothing substantial is ever built by waiting for the right time. We need it. Let's first each make a pledge ourselves, and immediately start the campaign."

1973 — Yeshivah students won top place in the Mishnayos and Berachah Contests. No father could have been more proud of the accomplishments of his own children than the Rabbi was in the accomplishments of the children of his yeshivah family.

1978 — Sunday before Pesach, 250 alumni of the yeshivah gathered to hear his *shiur* and enjoy the warmth of his company; the special pride when he saw "his" boys and girls return after learning in Eretz Yisrael.

1980 — Rosh Hashanah, the Rabbi, in great pain, walked to blow shofar for his mother. A few days later, on Yom Kippur, he was the *baal tefillah* for *Ne'ilah*. Question: "Rabbi, you're in such great pain. Why exert yourself?" His answer, "As long as one can, one should!"

In his last years, when "extremism" had become a lifestyle for many, the Rabbi's ability to keep to a predetermined "middle-of-the-road" course, made him stand out as an oasis of "balance." A "*masmid*" who offset his learning with "*l'maaseh*" — action; a dignitary whose entrance into any room conveyed the fact that a presence had arrived — yet, he could lower himself to pick up a scrap of paper in the yeshivah's hallway. He was a leader who would temper his power of enthusiasm and inspiration with his love and insistence for "seder" — order; an educator whose overriding desire to see every student reach their full potential was balanced by a realistic understanding that too much, too soon, too fast, will in the long run be educationally counterproductive.

Of all the many life values that I learned from the Rabbi, there are two educational philosophies I would like to mention. First, was the Rabbi's description on how to prepare a lesson or learn the *pasuk*, or "*limud*" a minimum of four time (here the Rabbi quoted a *Chazal*) and you then become so inspired by the "limud" that "it pours over to your students!" Like pouring wine into a cup until it flows over its rim, so too the *mechanech's* task is to be so saturated and enthused by the *limud* that it "overflows" into the heart of the talmid. Whereas teaching may mean presenting a lesson, *chinuch* means inspiring a *talmid*!

The second point was the Rabbi's deep belief in the resiliency of people and the invincibility of the Jewish *neshamah*. The Rabbi believed — and practiced daily — that every Jew, regardless of how far he may have wandered from the true path, with loving guidance could be brought back to the fold; every child, regardless of how "bad" he is, with loving direction can be made into an exemplary student.

Just as the superbly designed ship can right itself after being incessantly pounded by high waves, so too, integral in the *nishmas Yisrael* is the ability to "bounce back." Thus the person who at this moment may still be far from *Yiddishkeit* need only be shown a positive example; the couple whose marriage is disintegrating need only be given heartfelt guidance; the seemingly impossible student needs only direction and loving concern, and even an unbearable situation can be turned around.

This concept of "positive expectancy" filtered down from the Rabbi's office and affected every student in every class.

Who will ever know how many lost *neshamos* found their way back, how many families were saved, and how many potentially delinquent children straightened out and found meaning and purpose in their lives — because the Rabbi believed in them.

And then there are so many other ways to remember him — the warmth of his personality, his deep concern for all about him, his charismatic humor and princely social graces, his overwhelming respect for his mother, his devotion to his wife and family, his uncanny ability to make every *pasuk* come alive and be relevant to the present occasion, his happiness in doing a *mitzvah*, his special glow in doing "chesed" or giving *tzedakah*, his *simchas hachaim*, joy of living a full and purposeful life.

It has been said that an organization is the elongated shadow of one man. Rather than the word "shadow" I think that a more accurate description to personify the Rabbi's stamp on the students of the Yeshiva of Spring Valley in particular and the community of Monsey in general would be "light and joy." His life and teachings are the heritage he bequeathed to us.

Monsey is renowned the world over as the model of American Torah life. The Rabbi planted the seed, and for over 30 years the Rabbi tended this garden with love and compassion. He personally become the prototype of just such a Torah life serving Hashem and His children.

No memorial — regardless of how grandiose — will ever do justice to such a regal life. The army of Hashem's children who carry the indelible memory of the warmth and devotion of Rabbi Greenbaum — the Rabbi's "Life Values"— are truly the most fitting, most noble, most meaningful memorial any person can have.

ABOUT THE AUTHOR

Mr. Avi Shulman was a classroom teacher for over twenty-five years, National Director of Torah Umesorah's S.E.E.D. program, and currently teaches in Aish Dos and Mercaz teacher training programs.

He is the author of twenty personal-growth and parenting books and cassette programs, and writes a popular weekly column for Torah Umesorah published in the Yated Ne'eman.

Mr. Shulman is a nationally acclaimed speaker and teacher.

This volume is part of
THE ARTSCROLL SERIES®
an ongoing project of
translations, commentaries and expositions
on Scripture, Mishnah, Talmud, Halachah,
liturgy, history, the classic Rabbinic writings,
biographies and thought.

For a brochure of current publications
visit your local Hebrew bookseller
or contact the publisher:

Mesorah Publications, ltd.

4401 Second Avenue
Brooklyn, New York 11232
(718) 921-9000
www.artscroll.com